# you
### and your baby

**other titles in the You and Your Child Series**
Editor, Dr A. H. Brafman

**you and your toddler**
   Jenny Stoker
**you and your child:** making sense of learning disabilities
   Sheila and Martin Hollins

# you
# and your baby

## a baby's emotional life

*Frances Thomson Salo*

**You and Your Child Series**
Editor, Dr A. H. Brafman

Routledge
Taylor & Francis Group

LONDON AND NEW YORK

First published 2005 by Karnac Books

Published 2019 by Routledge
2 Park Square, Milton Park, Abingdon, Oxon OX14 4RN
52 Vanderbilt Avenue, New York, NY 10017

*Routledge is an imprint of the Taylor & Francis Group, an informa business*

**British Library Cataloguing in Publication Data**

A C.I.P. for this book is available from the British Library

Edited, designed, and produced by Communication Crafts

ISBN 13: 978-1-85575-363-1 (pbk)

to the parents and babies
who have helped me understand

# contents

*about the author*                                                                    xi

*acknowledgements*                                                                    xii

*series editor's foreword*                                                            xiii

1   setting the scene                                                                   1

**Primary maternal preoccupation**                                                      5
**A baby's mind seeks meaning**                                                         6
**The psychosomatic language**                                                          7
**Early anxieties**                                                                     7
**A loving parent inside**                                                              8
**Developing a sense of self**                                                          9
**Conclusion**                                                                         10

## I
## a baby's developing self

2   the developing self in the first two months                                        13

**What a baby brings**                                                                 13
**Being enjoyed**                                                                      17
**The interplay between the parents' and baby's contributions**                        18
**Co-constructing the parent–infant relationship**                                     21
**Conclusion**                                                                         23

| 3 | a baby's intentional self | 24 |
|---|---|---|
| | Primed to communicate | 24 |
| | Imitation | 26 |
| | Feeding | 27 |
| | Playfulness | 29 |
| | Crying as communication | 30 |
| | Relating in a threesome | 32 |
| | The second six months | 32 |
| | Frustration and saying "no" | 34 |
| | Walking | 35 |
| | Conclusion | 36 |

| 4 | a baby's self-recognition | 37 |
|---|---|---|
| | Self-comforting | 37 |
| | Smiling | 38 |
| | The psychosomatic body | 39 |
| | Self-consciousness | 40 |
| | Mapping and enjoying the body | 41 |
| | Differentiating self from other | 43 |
| | Temperament | 44 |
| | Self-esteem | 47 |
| | Complex relational feelings | 47 |
| | Hurt and shame | 49 |
| | Anxiety and fantasying | 50 |
| | Anger and ambivalence | 51 |
| | What babies need from their parents | 53 |
| | Holding babies' memories | 53 |
| | Conclusion | 54 |

| 5 | a baby's empathic self | 55 |
|---|---|---|
| | Developing expectancies | 56 |
| | Babies need their parents' thinking mind | 57 |
| | The language of the eyes | 58 |
| | Intersubjective communication of feelings | 60 |
| | Identification with others | 62 |
| | Teasing | 62 |
| | Gender differences in empathizing | 63 |
| | The achievements of the self | 64 |
| | Capacity to play alone | 64 |
| | Expressing feelings | 65 |
| | Conclusion | 65 |

## II
## the tasks facing the developing self

6 relating to fathers, siblings, and other people    69

Fathers    69
Siblings    72
Extended family    74
Other children    75
Conclusion    76

7 attachment and separation    77

The experience of separation    77
Secure and insecure attachment    79
Sleeping    81
Weaning and feeding difficulties    83
Transitional objects and activities    85
Stranger-anxiety    86
Helping with separation    87
Child care    87
Conclusion    88

8 thinking    89

Making the inner world more realistic and protecting it    89
Thinking    90
Sense of time    91
Understanding language    92
Conclusion    94

9 feeling good and feeling the best:
healthy narcissism and omnipotence    95

Feeling omnipotent and thinking magically    95
Consolidating self-esteem and narcissism    96
Conclusion    97

10 concern and oedipal wishes    98

Developing concern    98
Oedipal feelings    99
Difficulties in the oedipal stage    102
Beginnings of a value system or conscience    103
Conclusion    105

## III
## the self in difficulty

11   physical and emotional difficulties      109

**Pain, illness, or disability**      109
**When there are emotional difficulties**      111
**Adopted and fostered babies**      111
**Being born after a bereavement**      112
**Response to traumatic events**      112
**"Ghosts in the nursery"**      113
**Being with a mother who is depressed**      113
**Responding to trauma in the relationship**      115
**Coping in ways that constrict**      116
**Infant–parent psychotherapy**      118

afterword      121

*the search for ariadne's thread—the first year of life*
   *by Claus G. H. Newman*      123
*notes*      133
*index*      139

# about the author

Frances Thomson Salo is a psychoanalyst of adults and children. She has worked as a child psychotherapist in the public health services in the United Kingdom and Australia for nearly forty years. Her training as a psychoanalyst and her work as a child psychotherapist gave her a grounding in understanding how children communicate their feelings and their hope to be understood. Her work with parents experiencing difficulties in their babies' early years, coupled with her experience as a leader of over forty year-long infant observation seminars, consolidated her understanding of babies' subjective experience of the world. As well as her private practice, she is a Senior Lecturer on the University of Melbourne Graduate Diploma/ Masters in Parent and Infant Mental Health. She provides supervision to psychiatric registrars at the Royal Children's Hospital, Melbourne and to senior staff in local child and adolescent mental health services and child care services for children and adolescents and has been involved in the training of psychoanalysts and other mental health professionals. She has published a number of articles and chapters in the field of infancy and child psychotherapy and has co-edited several books, including (with Campbell Paul) *The Baby as Subject*.

# acknowledgements

Many babies and their parents, as well as many colleagues, have helped me to understand how babies develop. I am particularly grateful to Ann Morgan, Brigid Jordan, Sue Morse, and Michele Meehan—and, above all, to Campbell Paul of the Royal Children's Hospital in Melbourne, Australia—for their inspired clinical wisdom, which they shared so unstintingly. I am also grateful to those observers whose observations I refer to and whom, in order to protect the families' privacy, I have not named in person. My thanks also to Georgia Tucker for her comments on early drafts.

# series editor's foreword

Dr A. H. BRAFMAN

In this first volume of the You and Your Child Series, Frances Thomson Salo focuses on the main changes and challenges that occur during the year in which the child moves from birth to toddlerhood. Drawing on her great clinical experience, she considers in detail the developmental stages in those first twelve months and how these affect the baby's parents. We also have an overview of some relevant medical issues in this period as seen by an eminent paediatrician, Claus G. H. Newman.

There is a central philosophy uniting all the volumes in the You and Your Child Series. Each of the authors featured has published papers and books for the academic and clinical communities; the present volumes, however, are specifically aimed at parents. The intent is not to convince but to inform the reader. Rather than offering solutions, we are describing, explaining, and discussing the problems that parents meet while bringing up their children, from infancy through to adulthood.

We envisage that two groups of parents may choose to read these books: some may wish to find here answers to specific questions or to problems they are facing in their lives, whereas others may read them only to broaden their knowledge of human development. Our intention is that the writing should be phrased in a way that might satisfy both groups. There is an attempt at something of a translation of what children of different ages experience in their lives with parents, family, and the wider world. Our authors have based their texts on their extensive work with children, adolescents, and their parents—not only in the authors' private consulting-rooms, but also in schools, community agencies, and teaching hospitals—and, in most cases, with children of their own.

The authors aim to depict the child's experiential view of his life, helping parents to understand behaviours, thoughts, and feelings that the child may not have been able to verbalize. There is no question of being the child's advocate—no purpose is seen in trying to find who is to blame for the problems under discussion. These are, rather, interested and knowledgeable professionals attempting to get child and parents to understand each other's point of view. In our books, the authors describe in detail the increasing range of each child's developing abilities on the path from infancy to adulthood: it is this knowledge of potential and actual abilities that is fundamental for an understanding of a child's behaviour.

Many, if not most, of the books available on child development adopt the view that a child is the product of the environment in which he is brought up. To some extent, this is obviously true: the child will speak his parents' language and adopt the customs that characterize the culture in which the family live. The commonly heard remark that a particular child "takes after" a parent or other close relation bears out the fact that each growing individual responds and adapts to the milieu in which he lives—and not only in childhood, but throughout his life. Nevertheless, it is still true that not all children brought up in one particular home will show the same characteristics. From a scientific point of view, there are endless discussions on the issue of nature versus nurture. However, from a pragmatic point of view, it is certainly more correct and more useful to consider family problems with children as being the result of an interaction—who started this, and when and how it started, is

virtually impossible to establish. Through their words and behaviour, child and parents continually confirm each other's
expectations; they keep a vicious circle going, where each of
them feels totally justified in their views of themselves and of
each other.

It is not rare that the parents present quite different read-
ings of what each of them considers their child's problems to
be. Needless to say, the same can be found when considering
any single issue in the life of an ordinary family. The baby cries:
the mother thinks he is hungry, whereas the father may feel
that here is an early warning of a child who will wish to control
his parents' lives. The toddler refuses some particular food: the
mother resents this early sign of rebellion, whereas the father
will claim that the child is actually showing that he can discriminate between pleasant and undesirable flavours. The 5-year-old
demands a further hour of television watching: the mother
agrees that he should share a programme she happens to
enjoy, whereas the father explodes at the pointlessness of
trying to instil a sense of discipline in the house. By the time the
child has reached puberty or adolescence, these clashes are a
matter of daily routine. . . . From a practical point of view, it is
important to recognize that there is no question of ascertaining
which parent is right or which one is wrong: within their
personal frames of reference, they are both right. The problem
with such disagreements is that, whatever happens, the child
will always be agreeing with one of them and opposing the
other.

There is no doubt that each parent forms an individual
interpretation of the child's behaviour in line with his or her
own upbringing and personality, view of him/herself in the
world, and past and present experiences, some of them conscious and most of them unconscious. But—what about the
child in question? It is not part of ordinary family life that a
child should be asked for *his* explanation of the behaviour that
has led to the situation where the parents disagree on its

interpretation. Unfortunately, if he is asked, it can happen that he fails to find the words to explain himself, or occasionally he is driven to say what he believes the parent wants to hear, or at other times his words sound too illogical to be believed. The myth has somehow grown that in such circumstances only a professional will have the capacity to fathom out the child's "real" motives and intentions.

It is an obvious fact that each family will have its own style of approaching its child. It is simply unavoidable that each individual child will have his development influenced—not *determined* but *affected*—by the responses his behaviour brings out in his parents. It is, however, quite difficult for parents to appreciate the precise developmental abilities achieved by their child. No child can operate, cope with life, or respond to stimuli beyond his particular abilities at any particular point in time. And this is *the* point addressed in the present series of books. We try to provide portraits of the various stages in the child's cognitive, intellectual, and emotional development and how these unfolding stages affect not only the child's experience of himself, but also how he perceives and relates to the world in which he lives. Our hope is that establishing this context will help the parents who read these books to see their child from a different perspective.

## A note on the use of pronouns

In general discussions in this Series, for simplicity of language, masculine pronouns are used to denote the child and feminine pronouns the parent. Unless specified by the context, the word "parent" should be taken to mean mother, father, or other significant caregiver.

# you
### and **your baby**

# setting the scene

Babies want, more than anything else, to be enthusiastically enjoyed. That may seem an unexpected place to start, but it lies at the heart of how, as a psychoanalyst working with and observing babies and their families, I think about babies. Babies come into the world already knowing a lot, with a functioning mind primed to communicate and to learn quickly. Appreciating this is of fundamental importance for understanding babies.

This series of books was conceived partly as a resource for parents to gain some understanding of what their child is likely to be feeling. We cannot know exactly what a baby thinks and feels, but knowledge about how babies may experience their interaction with their parents is increasing exponentially. The great English paediatrician and psychoanalyst Donald Winnicott, who saw some 60,000 babies, believed that the answers to understanding their baby lay in the parents themselves. My hope is that understanding more about the exquisite capacities with which babies come into the world empowers their parents to feel that the answers are in them. Once we know how babies are capable at an early age of understanding and carrying out certain actions, we become, in turn, even more aware of their capacities. If parents can tune-in to how much their baby longs to connect with people, they might be fascinated to engage with and share their baby's fascination with them.

This book is for parents who are interested in understanding about their baby and about themselves. It is not a book with advice about physical and cognitive development (although I sometimes discuss this when it seems connected with a baby's emerging sense of self), nor is it about how to bring up babies. Rather, it is written in the belief that working out what to do follows more easily from understanding what babies are feeling and thinking.

The book brings together insights from working therapeutically with babies, children, and adults with those from infant research and from infant observation—long-term naturalistic observation of babies in their own homes. This kind of observation is undertaken as part of the training of child psychotherapists and psychoanalysts, and many helpful ways of knowing about babies have emerged as a result. I have drawn on some examples from observers for descriptions of babies' lives, although the examples cannot be comprehensive.

Writing as a clinician with nearly two decades' experience working with distressed babies and their families, I have attempted to integrate the different strands of knowledge in what I think is the most helpful way to understand babies. Understanding the attachment bond—the emotional relationship between babies and those who care for them—stems from observing behaviour. But this alone would not describe all the ways we have of thinking about a baby's mind. For that, we also need the fine-grained understanding that comes from seeing adults and children in psychoanalysis and psychotherapy. Having trained as a psychoanalyst and child psychotherapist, the most useful approach I have found in working with distressed infants and their families has been a distillation of a psychoanalytic approach and some of the findings from infant research.

I have focused on the baby's subjective experience of the world. If we put babies in central place, it follows that they are to be treated not as an object but as a subject in their own right. When we meet babies for the first time, we need to recognize and respect their subjectivity.

I have concentrated on the early months because they are often the hardest to understand. At times I may seem to speak for babies in a way that I cannot possibly know. Much of what a baby feels and thinks is preverbal, but we only have words to try to capture the essence of what we think the thoughts and feelings are. However, in the past, parents may have been silenced when academic psychology seemed to discount what parents intuitively felt they knew. Mothers talk to their babies as though they unconsciously feel that their babies understand them. The more we learn from neuroscientific research, the more likely it is that we are right to trust our intuition about what a baby feels.

I begin by describing some of the parents' feelings as they prepare for their baby; I then describe the beginning two months of their baby's life. What babies experience is presented first in terms of the three main ways in which the sense of self develops: *intentionality, recognition of their own body and feelings and those of other people,* and *empathy.* Parents may initially feel that ideas about the very young baby developing empathy may be a little far-fetched, but as some of these ideas are explored, parents usually find such ideas resonate for them, perhaps from a time when they themselves were babies. Chapters 3, 4, and 5 describe these strands of development taking place alongside one another, inextricably interconnected and unfolding in a chronological way from the second month onwards. In part II, I change the focus to look in more depth at how babies relate to their fathers, their siblings, and other people. The main achievements of the first year are also described, such as coping with separations, the development of thinking processes, the consolidation of self-esteem, and the development of concern for others. In the final part, I look briefly at what may happen when babies are ill or when unresolved emotional difficulties are revived for their parents.

I describe some of what parents' think and feel, as, particularly in the early months, there is such a reciprocal effect between their babies' minds and their own. While this book is more about understanding when development progresses well enough, I have indicated when there may be transient difficulties, to help parents think about the meaning of these for their babies and for them. When parents can be thoughtful about their babies, they are likely to have a sense of how to help with any difficulties that need attending to.

I have described babies who are cared for by their parents in a family home, whose development unfolds in an expectable way. Sometimes when I have referred to parents, it is implicit that this includes whoever is caring for the baby. I have not explored a baby's experience from the viewpoint of the different ways families are constituted nowadays. While there are also differences between cultures and how babies respond within their culture, these differences are probably smaller than might be expected, even when we compare patterns of childrearing in the Western world with those from cultures that do not emphasize individuality in the same way. Attachment theory, which underpins a considerable amount of current empirical research about babies, is not culturally specific, as it was originally derived in part from observations of mothers and babies in Uganda.

The ages given in the book are meant only as guides in capturing the achievements of the time periods. Because of what we now know about babies in their first year, it becomes hard to discuss a baby of this age without knowing precisely how old the baby is—the rate of development from the age of 1 day, to a week, to a month, to several months, to a year, is enormous.

It will be helpful when reading the subsequent chapters to have in mind the ideas outlined in the following sections.

## Primary maternal preoccupation

Towards the end of pregnancy and in the first few weeks after a baby's birth, the emotional world of the mother primarily revolves around feelings and thoughts about her baby.[1] In that dreamy, preoccupied state a mother loses herself, figuratively speaking, in order to get to know her baby. The mother of a 4-day-old baby said, stroking his forehead: "He is so beautiful. I sat here today for six hours, just looking at him." Babies need their mothers to help give them a sense of their bodies—where their bodies end and where others begin—a sense of their physical and emotional skin. A mother can be in touch with what her baby is feeling minute by minute, whereas other people are more outside this experience.

Primary maternal preoccupation lasts for several weeks after the birth of a baby. Mothers often talk about how, after the disorganization of the puerperium (the period between child-birth and the return of the altered anatomy, physiology, and biochemistry to the non-pregnant state), they feel that the identity they had before their baby's birth returns about two months after it. With a subsequent baby, the feelings may be just as intense, but a mother might not have the same amount of time to dwell on the new baby. Fathers may develop a preoccupation similar to the one that mothers develop. (One such father, who became forgetful about everyday matters, enquired whether there was a term to describe the fathers' condition, as there is for mothers'.)

When parents are able in pregnancy to integrate fantasies about their baby with those they have about their relationship as a couple, this has a positive effect on the quality of family interaction. Parents, particularly mothers, are faced with their tiny baby's total dependence on them; in some ways, this is hard, as very young babies have so few ways to give parents any feedback to reward them.

## A baby's mind seeks meaning

Babies are born with brains already "on-line" and actively seeking to make meaning out of their experience. Their brains, in turn, are partially structured by their experiences, but that does not mean that everything is fixed once and for all in the first year. Rather, their experiences act as a template through which their brains filter all subsequent experience and one that is capable of being modified with different experiences.[2] Babies who have strong relationships with those who care for them draw a resilience from this and remain open to subsequent experience.

Babies do not come into the world a blank slate; they come with their inherited potential. From the first moment, when they begin the process of coming to know themselves and discovering the outlines of their emerging self, they are acted on by the experiences they have. Their parents are simultaneously coming to know them and helping them know themselves.

Experiences in the first year are stored in the procedural memory system—the bodily memory system of ways-of-being with another person in the earliest years. These include the ways in which their parents comforted their distress. Memories in this system influence subsequent relationships, even though the memories are not subject to conscious recall. Many of the ways in which adults interact with babies come from procedural memory. If a baby experiences a traumatic event, the trauma is "remembered" by the body, which means that memories of difficult times are not completely lost but may show as a vulnerability. A baby who has been very frightened by an early experience usually retains traces of having been anxious.

Because babies attempt to make meaning out of everything, much of what they feel and do has meaning. We may not always understand their experience, but viewing babies in this way

helps keep the focus on their actions and behaviour as purposeful rather than random or inexplicable.

## The psychosomatic language

Babies have no way of communicating pain or distress apart
from crying or other bodily ways, such as sleeping difficulties or
feeding difficulties or other bodily upsets. As the psychosomatic language is the first language of a baby, disturbances for
which there is no organic cause express babies' emotional pain
or a pain shared with a parent. The more urgent psychosomatic
presentations occur when babies feel they can no longer hold
it together, as though an emotional skin is giving way. Some of
these ways of expressing distress continue throughout life: an
adolescent said that whenever she was stressed, her skin broke
out in a rash. Let us look at the different kinds of anxiety a baby
may feel.

## Early anxieties

Anxiety evolves gradually, from the panic that newborns may
experience to the more specific anxieties that children and
adults experience. Sometimes newborns look frightened, as
though they feel they might be dropped when they are passed
though space, as they have no way of knowing that someone is
holding them. The fear of falling into nothingness or being left
alone forever is, for the baby, an anxiety about annihilation, an
experience of "nameless dread".[3] These very early anxieties
may often be out of touch with reality. If adults experienced
these anxieties and were to catastrophize, "What if this were to
happen and this and this?", it would be easy to think they had
lost touch with reality. As everyone has experienced such anxi-

eties early in their life, these fears remain in our memories as a part that can lose touch with reality if they are re-evoked when caring for babies.

If babies or their parents are angry, this can create anxiety for the baby and disturb the smooth functioning of their relationship. Just as babies are angry at times about what they feel are deprivations in their relationship with their parents, so parents have many reasons for mixed feelings towards their baby and for being anxious about these feelings. The normal ambivalence in every relationship may cause them considerable grief.

The evolving anxieties that babies experience include fears of being separated from or abandoned by their parents, of being physically hurt, or of being disapproved of, shamed, and losing their parents' love. Conflicts between states of the self or conflict with the environment lead to anxiety and distress. Some babies feel very anxious about any change at all.

Babies respond to these early anxiety situations by trying to get rid of the bad feelings and discomfort. We think that they try self-protectively to split off the bad by imagining, "It's not in me, it's outside, and I only have good inside." They come to learn that some of what is good is outside, like their mother who comes to meet their needs, and some of what is bad and uncomfortable is inside. Babies need ways of protecting against anxiety, whether or not it is realistically based. Imagine an ongoing system in which a baby *projects* an idea or feeling outside, then takes it back, modified according to the reception it met in the outside world. This reality-testing helps to build up babies' inner world of mental representations of people who are important to them.

## A loving parent inside

The way parents love and care for their babies becomes part of how babies feel about themselves. The good experiences that they have in their first months help to build up a sense of loving, supportive internal parents as a life-long resource as well as an early sense of trust. Babies then have a sense that their parents are there for them and will love them unconditionally. Initially, to the baby it may feel like an actual presence accompanying him, before becoming more a way of looking after himself. Christina Noble, who suffered extreme abuse in her childhood after her mother died when she was 4 years old, was asked how she had the will to live, and she replied that it was due to her mother: "You see, I had love. I had a little, tiny foundation."[4]

The "good internal mother" is a representation, a way of thinking about the baby's experience of being mothered. When babies feel secure with a good mothering presence, they feel loving, hopeful, and creative. If a mother found it difficult to enjoy herself after the birth of her baby, she has refound an internal good mother once she begins to enjoy herself again. Mothers need mothers, and if a mother feels that she has not been deserted by her internal good mother, she will be tolerant of her mixed feelings towards herself and her baby and able to mother her baby better. She regains a perspective that she will not be stuck forever with infinitely depressing feelings. Caring and having fun are creative activities.

The concept of a good internal mother overlaps with the theory of secure attachment. The inner security described above is what most babies experience in their relationship with their parents. (There is more about this in chapter 7.)

## Developing a sense of self

The developing self begins to emerge from the different experiences a baby has. A baby's self is his unique identity that exists over time and space and includes the sense of being a causal agent and of having a certain gender. An evocative idea is that of each baby's true or authentic self.[5] Parents try to find this in each baby, feeling that each baby is special in his own right.

A baby's gender is an important part of the self. Parents gender their baby from birth onwards and respond differently physically and verbally to male and female babies, usually engaging in more active physical games with their sons than with their daughters. Parents both respond to and shape innate sex differences between female and male babies from the first days. One-day-old girl babies cry more intensely at the sound of other babies crying than do boy babies. And there are differences in social interest: 1-day-old girl babies look longer at a face, and boy babies longer at a mobile. Male babies seem to need their parents' help in soothing their distress and regulating their emotional and physical states more than do female babies. Accumulating evidence suggests that boys seem from the beginning to be better at understanding and organizing systems, and girls seem to be more empathic.[6] This is not to suggest that these traits belong exclusively to either sex but, rather, that there are some general differences.

We need to not forget that the meaning of behaviour may change from one week to the next or within an even shorter space of time. The factors that initially led to a baby's crying may not be the factors that keep it going. A little baby's gag reflex may mean that milk is vomited up easily, but if milk and food continue to be vomited up frequently there may be a number of reasons for this, some of them physical and some emotional.

## Conclusion

With these ideas as a backdrop—of how the baby seeks meaning and responds to early anxieties through the psychosomatic language towards developing a good internal mother—let us look at what happens when babies meet their parents and they start getting to know each other.

## part I

# A BABY'S DEVELOPING SELF

". . . [a baby] cannot stop the vivid present to think"
W. H. Auden[1]

In part I, we look at the unfolding timetable of babies' capacities and, in particular, three aspects: the intentionality of babies' activity, how they come to recognize their bodies and feelings and differentiate them from other people's, and how they develop empathy.

# 2

## the developing self
## in the first two months

Babies come into the world with exquisite capacities and are primed, hard–wired, to communicate with their parents and other people. They have a drive towards completing development, including a drive towards developing a self.

## What a baby brings

Even before birth, babies are aware of their mother's voice, feelings, and activities. They can hear, taste, and respond to pressure and touch, and they react to painful stimuli by moving away. About two months before they are born, they are aware of a rose-coloured light through the thinly stretched wall of their mother's abdomen during the day. Babies therefore come into the world with some cognitive and emotional knowledge of their parents.

Newborns are actively processing from birth onwards and know that they are separate. They can recognize their mother's face and voice from birth. They match up the sight of her face as she speaks to them with the sounds they have heard her make while they were in the womb. Some babies lock onto their mother's eyes in the delivery-room as if feeling that this is someone already known to them. Within the first hour they can turn to track their parent's voice, even if the parent is on the other side of the room. They can synchronize hand movements to syllables of adult speech in any language[1] and imitate an adult's facial gestures, such as mouth opening, and also finger movements. If an adult puts his or her tongue out, a baby usually imitates the gesture. The baby will repeat the imitative gesture even up to two minutes later to encourage the adult to do it again and re-engage with the baby. When babies are imitating, their heartbeat increases, and when they are inviting the adult to reciprocate, it slows.[2] Imitating helps babies be more attuned to their mothers and more alert.

Babies are born able to respond to experiences with a range of feelings. Newborns have a "sensitive and joyful appreciation of expression in the human voice".[3] Irrespective of the culture, they show the same expressions of interest, joy, distress, disgust, and surprise. They want to be involved with other people in order to share experiences with them. They try, almost from the beginning, to be meaningful to those who are important to them. They have a need to matter to others and to be kept in mind.

There are innate mechanisms that allow babies to attribute mental states to other people. Newborns, with their minds mirroring other minds, feel in their body what they see another person do and therefore feel that the other person is like them.[4] This forms a basis for intersubjectivity—that is, the capacity to understand and communicate mental states and to share subjective experience. When babies explore the environment they register proprioceptive information (i.e. the effect produced in them) at the same time, so that in exploring objects they are also exploring themselves.

An important task in the first six weeks or so is for babies, with their parents' help, to learn to self-regulate: to become familiar with their body and bring the different bodily systems more under their control. That is particularly important for those babies who are hypersensitive or dysregulated in their responses or, at the other end of the spectrum, who are slow to respond. Parents are often provided with guidelines, such as how much a baby should eat and sleep, that seem to overlook a baby's individuality and replace it with statements about what a baby should and should not be doing. Feeling that they need to adhere to these guidelines to be a good parent, parents may then make them part of the expectations with which they meet their baby. Rigidly following, for example, a guideline that babies need a certain number of hours of sleep may get in the way of parents seeing what their own baby actually needs. Being able to start from the viewpoint of their baby as an individual helps parents to observe and discern the evolving pattern of their baby's states and rhythms and guides them in helping their baby feel more settled. Some babies, for example, go to sleep happily mouthing their fist but startle very easily, so that it is difficult for them to keep their hand near their mouth. Arranging the bedclothes so that babies can more easily keep their hand near their mouth helps consolidate recognition of that baby's response pattern. Some parents notice that as their babies visually track objects they become calmer, so that having something patterned inside their cot helps them settle.

Babies gradually feel that experiences, as they get repeated, are linked, whether they happen inside or outside them. They have an experience of a "now" moment and then another one. This might be like, "That happened to me before", or, "I've been here before". Babies have a sense of coming into being, perhaps like a light bulb coming on and illuminating. In time, babies feel that a thread connects experiences, and gradually they have some sense of linking and continuity. A 3-week-old baby made a connection between his toy tiger and the striped T-shirt a visitor was wearing. When he looked at his tiger, his eyes became alert and he smiled. He then caught sight of the visitor's top and, smiling, looked backwards and forwards between that and the tiger.

Very early, babies can transfer information that they have learned in one sensory mode of perception to another. Three-week-old babies who were given either a smooth or a nubbly dummy to suck, but could not see the dummy, stared significantly longer at the picture of the one they had sucked once the dummies were removed and they were shown pictures of both kinds.[5] They had connected something felt but unseen with its seen representation. Rapid complex mental development is taking place, and the finding that 5-day-old babies are sensitive to number has led to claims that they can do mental arithmetic! (In one study, babies were shown an object until they were bored. The object was then covered with a screen, and if when the screen was removed the same object was there, the babies were soon bored again. If, however, two or three objects had been secretly placed there, the babies were surprised and stared longer at them.)

By 6 weeks of age, babies can both *remember* a stranger whom they saw the day before and reproduce unprompted an action that the stranger made then, inviting the stranger to engage with them.[6] Already at this age, babies have a considerable memory of those experiences they find interesting. By the time they are 2 months old, babies will, when adults change their focus of attention, readjust their gaze, understanding that the adults' gaze has moved to other objects that exist in a space held in common with other people and entering into a "communicative network".[7,8]

If at times babies feel overwhelmed by anxieties, how do they respond? They may show signs from the earliest days of remembering things that make them anxious. If during a breastfeed their airways were blocked, making it difficult to breathe, they may become anxious at subsequent feeds and hold back from the breast. And just as adults drop their gaze when something is painful to look at or makes them anxious, or they are trying to protect the other person from their anger, babies do the same. When babies feel overwhelmed or are anxious about their angry feelings, they look away so as not to meet their parents' eyes. It has the effect of denying and getting rid of something unwelcome. It is the best defence they can manage to protect their attachment ties when they feel that something in the relationship threatens to disrupt them.

Babies' drive towards mastery is closely connected with the tendency to convert passively endured experiences into something more active. This developmental principle lies behind many of their coping and defensive strategies. Later on, children play out experiences when they have felt helpless, like putting a Band-Aid on a teddy after being hurt.

## Being enjoyed

The world of the baby is interactive from the start. From birth onwards, babies want above all to be enthusiastically enjoyed by their parents and by other people who matter to them, and this is captured in the phrase "only connect".[9] They want the company of other lively human beings. Toddlers clearly let us know that it usually feels more of an achievement or fun when somebody else is acknowledging or praising them. Feeling cherished is a basis for developing empathy for the self and others.

Parents intuitively feel that their baby's early smiles have meaning and are intentional. Babies can smile within five days of being born. They quickly show their pleasure not just in smiles but in whole body movements of excitement that reward their parents. As they smile, these euphoric states are the most compelling for human beings. When a 7-week-old boy smiled at his mother, he was in raptures, his face glowed, his eyes twinkled, and he seemed in love with her. He gave her a knowing look, as if knowing why she was there and that he was safe.

By age 2 months, babies will try to re-engage their parents' attention, and by 3 months they call for attention when their parents are not there. Wanting to be enjoyed by other people is such a powerful motive that when babies feel enjoyed, there are few battles between parent and baby. The more that unnecessary battles are avoided, by humour or diversion, the more likely a baby is to have a positive sense of self and good self-esteem.

Conversely, babies are acutely sensitive to unresponsive facial expressions, which feel to them like the withdrawal of love. If a mother of a 6-week-old baby interrupts being playful with her baby to keep a *still face* for a minute, the baby is disconcerted, as if what the baby expected to happen had not happened. When the baby's mother relates normally again, the baby looks sad and may cry, as though hurt by what she did. What babies want is to feel that they are held in their parents' mind.

## The interplay between the parents' and baby's contributions

### Parents' contribution

Parents' bring their life histories, their dreams, and their expectations to meet their baby—who comes with his own temperament and other constitutional givens—and together they co-create a relationship. The parents' feelings include not just the separate well-known ones of joy and sadness, but also the background feelings of being tired, relaxed, or energized with which they carry out actions. Each day babies send out communicative feelers, to which their parents respond with emotional mutuality about 30% of the time that they interact face-to-face,[10] which is enough for babies to develop well.

Parents' capacity to understand their baby's nonverbal communication is extremely important. At least 60% of communication of all may be nonverbal. When things go well, parents intuitively read and understand their baby's communication, partly because they were babies once and human beings are hard-wired to read nonverbal communication. People process emotional messages within milliseconds, outside conscious knowledge. As mothers respond to their babies within one-twelfth of a second and babies respond nearly as quickly, this interaction truly deserves the description of a split-second world.[11] Babies can have incredibly responsive eyes, and there is no mistaking the communication they make. Five-week-old babies "drink" in their mother and try to engage their parents in a highly enjoyable wordless communion.

## Parents' attributions

The investment that parents have in their new baby is usually enormous. Their newborn baby looks the most perfect baby ever born. This *narcissism* vested in their baby allows a mother to parent her baby twenty-four hours a day in the beginning. Like a double-edged sword, however, mothers usually blame themselves for everything that is felt to go wrong—or that they fear might go wrong—with their baby.

Parents may read all kinds of thoughts and feelings into the way their baby is or behaves. They attribute likenesses to other family members or significant people. These *projections* onto their baby are both positive and negative, and some of these help new parents get to know their baby. As childbirth opens the door to the past, it can also let in these "ghosts".

Parents usually struggle with acknowledging their *ambivalence.* Whatever the hopeful emotions of joy and elation, parents at times feel guilty about their anger and hate. A mother fears that she will lose her sense of self and, at an unconscious level, feels that she is faced with a choice between her life and her baby's. Winnicott listed nearly twenty reasons why mothers *hate* their babies, such as that their babies will eat, smile, and sleep for other people and not do so for their mothers.[12] He wrote evocatively that, "The most remarkable thing about a mother is her ability to be hurt so much by her baby and to hate so much without paying the child out, and her ability to wait for rewards that may or may not come at a later date."

Parents, in thinking about how babies may be affected by the interaction with them, may feel that they are being blamed, whereas the approach that I advocate is, rather, one of trying to understand all the influences acting on babies, both from their own temperament and from their parents' unique life histories. When parents have more awareness of these influences, it may increase options for dealing with them. Once interactions start between parents and their babies, these have a bi-directional effect, so that each is shaped by the other. Each developmental achievement of the baby changes the nature of the parent–baby relationship.

The recognition that babies have a mind of their own and are their own person signals a new emotional separation. As a mother's idealized view of her baby develops into being a more realistic one, this helps her if she has found it hard to relinquish being very preoccupied with her baby.

Babies need their parents to be open to their feelings and allow them to resonate, so that the parents empathize with— but are not be overwhelmed by—them and are still able to think. When babies are troubled, it is not easy for their parents to be reflective. Babies need their distress to get through to their parents so that they can take effective action, but without feeling too jangled and stirred up.

A baby is often quickly aware if his parents are sad or anxious and has little escape when the feelings are very strong. While the mother of an 8-day-old baby talked of a miscarriage, his face crumpled with audible sobs in his sleep. A 9-week-old baby girl, who two weeks earlier had been very confident in the company of her placid older sister, sensed her mother's anxiety that the sister might hurt her and became scared of her. A 4-week-old boy who did not feel emotionally held by his mother held his head up incredibly sturdily as if he needed to be precociously independent, and similarly some 3½-month-old babies have been described as being like little warriors.

One difficulty that parents may experience is their own fear of babies, which everyone may have deep down, sometimes as a result of having had moments of feeling panicky as a baby. It is possible that traumatic experiences from the parents' past which have not been resolved may be resonated, like ghosts rising up from the past. Sometimes babies remind parents of someone about whom they had very troubled feelings, whether it was a sibling or an adult who in some way frightened them, or of another baby who has died. The baby may remind the parents of a part of their self which they do not feel good about; or the baby may have been born ill or disabled, which complicates how the parents feel about the baby. Babies then collect these feelings as they are projected onto them, and these can interfere with parents getting to know their baby.

These attributions or fantasies on the parents' part may make it harder for them to see their baby accurately and to think about creative solutions. That unrealistic views of a baby may take on a life of their own needs to be emphasized, as these may shape the baby's behaviour so that negative views get confirmed. It is hard for babies to escape this shaping, and they may comply or give up trying to wriggle out of a stereotyped way of being seen. Parents may also inadvertently get caught in this trap, because how they already see the baby influences what they focus on, so that it confirms rather than disconfirms their view of their baby.

## Co-constructing the parent–infant relationship

Parents give meaning to their baby's experience. They respond to a movement of their baby's head as a gesture meaning that the baby does not want a coat on, or to babbling as the baby telling them a story. Parents help to create a gap between themselves and their baby so that playing and independent thinking can flower.

Babies who in the first six months are comforted when they are distressed tend to be babies who, far from being spoiled, are happier and more settled in the second six months. Their parents have met their needs in such a way that they start to be confident that their needs will be responded to. When things go well, this increases positive feedback between parents and babies. If mothers or their babies express feelings that diverge too much from the other, within a couple of seconds one or other of them will try to match their expression more closely with that of the other. They are repairing a distance that is felt to be too great. These repairs can enrich their way of being together, as babies come to trust their parents' capacity to repair ruptures.

Babies need their parents to hang in there for the first couple of months while they get themselves together, and the rewards for parenting them become more evident after that. Paradoxically this may get harder for the parents if a baby's sleeping patterns do not settle down: the parents' sleep deprivation may be enough to make them depressed, even in the absence of personal or environmental reasons.

Often difficulties that belong *in* the relationship rather than just to the parents or their baby may be expressed by the baby not sleeping or eating well or being irritable. Or babies may become compliant as early as 3 weeks, as if sensing that they need to be very good. A 7-week-old boy used to "go away" in his eyes; they were vacant, as a survival mechanism to manage both his awareness that his parents did not have him in mind and his discomfort when his siblings were rough with him. When he felt he had his own place in his mother's mind, he did not need to do this.

## Conclusion

Babies bring considerable capacities to meet the world, and they relate from the outset. The primary wish of babies is to be enjoyed and to matter to those who care for them. When things go well and their anxieties are responded to sensitively, a secure attachment grows, linked with secure self-esteem.

# 3

## a baby's intentional self

When babies experience a sense of pleasurable mastery, this contributes to their sense of agency and to viewing themselves as an agentive self—as one who can cause things to happen. By age 12 weeks if not earlier, babies have learned about cause and effect in the external environment, but they have also been learning this about themselves since much earlier.

## Primed to communicate

The phrase *primed to communicate* captures an important aspect about babies. Babies have a capacity for primary intersubjectivity, to recognize another person as a distinct subject.[2] To facilitate this, they have the capacity to communicate from birth. Within the first two months, babies, when face to face with an adult who is talking to them, make lip and tongue movements similar to those the adult makes and respond with coos and murmurs as well as with expressive head, eye, and hand movements. By age 2-months, babies often "point" with their index finger as part of this.[3] Videotapes of mother–baby interactions show the gaze of mother and baby interlocking and their expressions mirroring one another. As a mother moves her head one way, her baby follows; as she moves it another way, her baby does, too. Second by second, she influences her baby and her baby influences her. Mother and baby seem to want to lose themselves in communication with one another, with no other purpose than to do just that.

"Emotional communication is supremely important in the development of the brain."[4] Let me try to explain that. As babies experience a range of feelings and attempt to make meaning out of them, neural and emotional connections open up for them.

One of the ways babies know who they are comes from their actions. From birth onwards, many of their actions convey a sense of intentionality. Their sense of agency conveys to them that they have a unique individual self. When babies immediately after delivery look at their mother with a long focused gaze, they powerfully convey that they feel they are at last meeting someone whom they have known for a long time in a different way. Babies can gaze at their parents in such a way that their parents feel that their babies are in some way thinking or fantasying.

After the first two months, the repertoire of intentional actions that babies have becomes much more extensive. A quick count includes gaze, physical activities, and spontaneous, enjoyable play. Being able to soothe themselves when distressed, which starts in the first two months, becomes more intentional and more clearly effective. From their actions, we think of them much more as a person. A 9-week-old girl gazed at a mobile and then at her mother, and everyone watching was convinced that she wanted her to turn it on. When her mother put her in a visitor's arms, she signalled clearly in her gestures and gaze, "You're the one I want. Don't put me in any one else's arms."

An observer described an 8-week-old boy engaged in conversation with her. He stuck his tongue out continuously for about three minutes, and they copied each other. He seemed to try to tell her things. He flapped his arms around, wiggled his body, and made short hooting noises. His expression was one of great wonder, eyebrows raised, eyes wide and bright, lips pursed. He continued this for about three minutes. She responded, and the tone of their voices was in rhythm. Occasionally he looked seriously at her and lowered his tone. He waited for her to finish what she said and at times looked intently at her eyes and lips. When she was quiet, he made another sound and maintained eye contact. He often smiled and turned his head to the side for a second, as though shy. When he had had enough, he began to frown, made growling noises, and turned to avoid her face.

## Imitation

Babies imitate intentionally from day one, as a bridge connecting self and other.[5] Babies start by imitating an adult's facial gestures, and as they imitate they find out more about what the other person feels or intends when they see what the other person does. What babies gradually learn is that, "When you imitate me you reflect back a bit of my self, but from inside it does not feel exactly the same. In that way I know I am different from you, and each time you and I imitate each other I learn a little more about what I feel." Babies want to be sociable and they want to share experiences. After 2 months of age, they also add gestures to see if they will be copied. It has become a matching game, and they soon become joyful when others join in a game of imitating. When babies imitate, they are clearly communicating with interest, pleasure, and surprise.

## Feeding

It may feel poetic to think that even at the first feed babies make a contribution to their mothers out of their innate creative potential. But the baby *is* giving something, in that with a good breastfeed not only is the baby having a feed but the baby's mother is too, in feeling that her baby is giving her something and helping her to become a mother.

As babies derive not only milk but also comfort from the breast or feeding situation, feeding quickly becomes linked with the bond between mother and baby. When things go smoothly during feeding, this helps to consolidate the babies' feeling that the world is safe and pleasurable to interact with, so it could be said that their mood determines what they do with their mouth. By about age 3 months, babies can tolerate there being a space between a feed at one breast and a feed at the other, as though they feel less anxious about separation and more confident of having a good mother inside them. By the same age they can often be seen to make a choice of whether they want to drink or whether they want to play and have fun with the nipple. A 4-month-old boy repeatedly caressed the breast slowly with a cupped hand and then explored it in a much faster way with an outstretched palm. Another boy the same age so enjoyed the introduction of solid food that he excitedly anticipated the next feed. When the food came, he leant forward with his arms and legs as though he wanted to embrace the experience with his whole body. Feeding patterns are suggestive of how babies may subsequently relate to the world, such as whether they are receptive to taking in knowledge and experiences.

Babies can also initiate some changes to shape the feeding:

A 6-week-old boy held his mouth open around the breast and touched it gently a few times with his lips, as though playing with the nipple. He sucked in a slow rhythmic way, gazing in a focused way at his mother, as though he felt, "This is my Mum". He held the breast almost as though he were caressing it, and his loving feelings for his mother were clear. By age 14 weeks, he turned his face away from her until she stood up to feed him out of reach of his siblings and would not feed unless she was really thinking about him. When he began to go to sleep she tried to remove her nipple, but he held on so tight it stretched, as if he wanted to keep it till he was ready to give it up and partly felt that the breast was his possession. When he was 18 weeks old, he no longer needed her to stand up. There was a confidence about the way he held the breast that he knew he was in her mind and would not be forgotten when she talked to his siblings. He connected easily with the breast in a different way, sitting up more, and his hands touched it almost as though he was holding it. When she offered him the other breast, he touched her skin around the nipple. He knew it was his mother's breast and seemed to have a relationship with the breast as separate from himself, and to be joining in too. When his hands curled over and held her hand for quite a long time, it had a sense of loving gratitude.

During the second half of the year, many babies try to feed themselves. The more parents can work with the baby's wish to be active, as in sitting upright and in having control of finger food, the better this is likely to go. While the spoon comes from outside, once it is inside the mouth it feels like it is the baby's possession. Babies vary enormously as to how long they will persevere with tastes they are not keen on. Some babies who are used to the continuous flow of milk do not like the stopping and starting of spoonfeeding and might shut their mouths on the spoon till they feel they have regained a sense of equilibrium.

Towards the end of the first year, babies reciprocate their parents' spoonfeeding—a baby will offer food to his parent's mouth and open his own mouth just as his parent unconsciously opened her mouth when feeding him.

When babies have a sense of autonomy and pleasure about feeding, it lessens the possibility that there will be problems. However, when babies have negative reactions so that their sense of mastery and pleasure at this interface with the world is affected, taking in information or a "good feed" such as a compliment may be difficult. (Weaning and feeding difficulties are discussed further in chapter 7.)

## Playfulness

A baby's playfulness can be seen in the first two months. Play is innately creative, with an enormous potential for communication. Joining in a baby's play often gives something back to parents, taking them into a magical world of pleasure in a way that they might not have expected; it becomes a "dance" between the two partners.

Some mothers feel that their baby is very playful with the nipple, playing at pushing it away then stretching it and sucking it in. Babies enjoy experiences of interactive play with another adult or baby from just a few weeks of age. Two-month-old babies can anticipate what will happen next in a bouncing game, so already they have a representation of the self and the other person.

> While her mother worked in the next room, a 5-month-old girl played for fifteen minutes in a completely self-motivated way, knowing what she wanted and sometimes interacting with her observer. First, she reached out doggedly to get some toys. When she sat up, she grabbed the play frame to her mouth and sucked the toys. She banged toys together with rings and had fun with them. She chatted away, looking at the observer. It was as though the rings were her creation. She flicked them and twice hit herself but was not deterred. She conveyed the development of a sense of self from the way the play arose from within her, in an undriven and pleasurable way.

Some babies play in a symbolic way towards the end of the first year. An 8-month-old girl put her doll to her chest to breastfeed it. By age 11 months, babies can use symbolic play to explore cross and sad feelings.

An 11-month-old boy sat next to his observer, quietly giving her some dolls and hitting them to show her what he wanted her to do. Then he took two funnels, which were pink and round-cupped, sucked on the big one and blew through it, making a noise. He crawled over to his mother and, holding it in his mouth, blew it at her, and she said he was playing it like she had earlier played the clarinet. He looked very pleased with himself as he made the noise. When she played her clarinet, he smiled broadly and held on to her. He went back to the toys which he handed to the observer, patting them so that she would too, and listening as they made a noise. His mother thought that he had played in this way because he knew the observer was about to stop visiting.

## Crying as communication

Tiny babies can express and communicate pain or distress only through crying or in other bodily ways. Very quickly their crying carries their feelings of hunger, tiredness, unhappiness, boredom, confusion, or fright. Five-week-old babies can yell with furious rage about having to wait for a feed when they are hungry. Babies are learning at this time to regulate themselves, and their parents are learning too. Babies respond differently to their own internal experiences, as some can wait confidently for a feed whereas others cannot. Some babies who get very frightened about the normal physiological processes taking place inside them overreact, and their crying reflects this. It is useful to map babies' emotional responses to internal and external experiences and to how babies begin to make links between their distress and how their parents attend to it.[6]

Parents' capacity to tune into the emotional feelings that their baby evokes in them is one of the most reliable ways of reading their baby's cues. We do not always know the meaning of a baby's crying, but holding him close when he is distressed lets him know his parents are nearby. Keeping their baby close and carefully observing his individual behavioural cues may help parents understand better the reason for the crying. The baby may, for example, be crying not to be fed but to be picked up. When parents are relaxed, their sensitivity to the baby increases and they become better at comforting the baby and easing the crying.

Sometimes babies may not have been able to get the message through to their parents that by about 6 weeks, their crying is because they are alert and do not need to be treated as if they are in a cocoon and should only sleep. Alert, aware babies may find it very hard to cope if they feel there is not enough to keep them interested.

How do we understand why babies' crying often lessens at around age 3 months? The crying that is often referred to as 3-month colic probably stems from a number of reasons. The answer seems to lie somewhere between babies' physical bodies maturing, in combination with their being able to regulate themselves better, and their parents feeling more confident about understanding their baby better.

Often the difficulty adults have in listening to a baby cry—some people say they hate it—is one reason they tune out. Sometimes when they have not been able to relieve a baby's distress despite trying very hard to do so, the crying feels unbearable. Continued crying, particularly when babies do not get enjoyment from their play at other times, is a communication that something is not right and that help is needed (see chapter 11).

## Relating in a threesome

From age 2 months onwards, babies enjoy watching their parents interact. From 3 months onwards, when babies are interacting with one person they increasingly reach out with gestures and vocalizations to include a third person. This has been called triadic intersubjective communication. Being effective at this communication reinforces babies' sense of efficacy.

Towards the end of the first year, a baby in the presence of another baby and an adult will continue to be interested in both of them, even if the adult turns to the other baby, and will also direct actions towards both of them. A 9-month-old boy seemed to recognize that a younger baby felt less socially capable, and he acted affably, leaning towards her, waving both arms up and down, with a long, wide-open smile and raised eyebrows.[7]

## The second six months

In the second six months, a baby's intentionality is much clearer. The pleasure babies have in exploring and practising infuses all their motor activity, particularly crawling, pulling themselves up, and starting to walk. The "scientist in the crib" of this period is endlessly curious and ceaselessly exploring. Babies work things out by connecting pieces of information to try to understand the world. A 6-month-old girl sitting in her playpen saw a toy that she wanted on the far end of a towel that stretched from the playpen quite a distance away. Slowly, over several minutes, she pulled the towel inch-by-inch closer until she could reach the toy. A month later, she tried to fit the lid of a toy back onto it.

Developments in the arena of feelings, thoughts, and intentions shared between babies and their parents include intentional communication, even jokes. Not only do babies want to share an experience—adults, too, want to point at something, share the feelings, and ask, "What do you think of it?" A 6-month-old child used to make a particular sound as if trying to make her parents laugh again. Another one touched her mother's nipple and her own nose and found this hilarious, as though she thought it was a joke.

During times of shared attention, mother and baby gaze at the same thing together, often switching gaze between the object and each other. They may also vocalize, smile, and touch each other, and increasingly from 6 months onwards the games babies and parents play together include objects, with babies trying playfully to put them in the parents' mouths. All this helps babies to develop a sense of shared feelings and understanding of other minds. Their ability to have a joint focus of attention and shared feelings with other people makes it possible for them to move away from their parents because the sharing can sustain them.

A 7-month-old girl used the health visitor's gaze for most of an hour's visit to hold herself together when her mother was very sad and tense. When the health visitor inadvertently stepped out of the baby's vision, she cried out in protest, so the health visitor stepped back; when the baby saw her face, she stopped crying. She watched the health visitor intently, without smiling or vocalizing, and when her mother moved her she cried, swivelled round on her tummy, and lifted her head to see the health visitor. If the health visitor turned her head to talk to the mother, the baby made an urgent-sounding vocalization calling her back. She did not initiate any playing and continued just looking into the health visitor's eyes. Her mother said soon after, "I just sit and watch her like you do, and now she's sleeping better."

By the end of the first year, babies take part in complex social games with unfamiliar adults and other babies and share toys with them spontaneously. They express themselves in more forceful ways and might remove an object from the lap of another baby's mother when they know the object belongs to the other baby. They sometimes use force against other babies whom they know, pulling their hair or biting them when they want something very much or are frustrated.

## Frustration and saying "no"

Gradually over the first few months, as babies become more aware of the gap between what they want to do and their capacity to fulfil it, they experience frustration. Their gladness when they are successful turns to disappointment or irritation at failure. A 6-month-old girl was grumpy when she was frustrated and slapped her thigh as if she did not know what to do with herself. She was also angry, because even when crying she did not put her arms out to her mother or cuddle into her. She seemed to try to get away from her mother, almost leaping out of her grasp as if she was bored sitting on her lap. But she was frustrated, as though aware that she could not get where she wanted to go.

In the second six months, it becomes clearer when a baby is saying "no". Previously when babies wanted to say no they turned their head away or pushed things away with their hands. Now they begin to shake their head in a side-to side motion. Saying no is a forerunner to the tantrums through which babies increasingly find their autonomy and independence. It is also a forerunner to saying no to the self—for example, being able to delay gratification when necessary.

When babies' parents are able to let them experience manageable frustration, this helps give the babies the opportunity to learn to deal with frustration. Babies need to learn they can survive the feelings aroused by limit setting. If, for example, a baby starts biting the breast towards the end of the first year, a gentle but firm "no, that hurts" helps them to start learning where the limits lie. Babies who find every wish gratified may later respond in angry ways to test the limits, or because they feel anxious. Babies who are easily frustrated may find it hard to develop ways that could help them alleviate their distress, which in turn might lead to difficulties with impulsivity and aggression. Some babies who have bouts of negativity try to get their parents to intervene, which makes it challenging for their parents to respond sensitively. When babies are very negative, their mothers often do more for them to prevent them becoming frustrated and difficult, whereas what such babies need to learn is how to take over the regulating for themselves. For such babies, learning to relax and wait when something is not forthcoming the moment they want it is very important.

Some babies, in their frustration, find more extreme ways in which they try to express and master their frustration, such as banging their head on a hard surface. It is as though this both expresses an internal pain and tries to get rid of it. As babies repeat this, it may become a habit. If parents have a sense that their baby does it when anxious or angry, this helps them find the most helpful way to address it, by talking about what he may be feeling and letting him know in the way that they hold and talk to him that they do not want him to be hurt. When parents tune into the meaning of it and reassure their babies, the head-banging does not need to become a fixed habit.

When babies find their frustration at the mismatches between their parents and themselves is too great, they may by 9 months try to protect themselves from the distress of this (see chapter 11).

## Walking

Babies may be walking or almost walking by the end of the first year. This changes things for them so much that it is like a discontinuity of experience. They see objects from a different perspective. With their locomotion now much more under their control, at times it feels frightening to put a distance between their parents and themselves. As they practise, from about 9 months onwards, crawling, pulling themselves up, and walking, their capacity to self-regulate is more in the foreground. At other times, the mutual regulation with their parents serves to refuel the energy and exuberance they have spent, though they may not need to physically touch base—it may be enough to glance in their parents' direction.

## Conclusion

Babies' intentional achievements reinforce their sense of themselves as agentive. When their actions have been effective, they develop a sense of themselves as effective. From that springboard of safety they enjoy exploring and taking risks, not because they are bored but because they welcome the liveliness in this.

# 4

## a baby's self-recognition

The roots of the self are in the body, in being conscious and recognizing feelings. Babies know who they are by recognizing their bodies as different from those of other people and by recognizing their own feelings—that they have experienced them before and remember what they felt like. It is impossible not to be experiencing feelings all the time, even if we are not aware of them.

Once babies know that, for example, their mother is the same person whether she has a happy face or a sad or surprised one, they have a coherent view of her as another person. When they see parts of their own body from different positions, whether sitting or lying, and know that they are the same person, they have a coherent view of themselves. Babies of 5 months of age respond to their name, as they can to their reflection in the mirror.

## Self-comforting

As babies become familiar with how their body works, they learn how to settle, to get pleasure from their body, and to feel good. They come to trust that their body will find its own rhythms (in the way that their parents also come to trust that their baby's body will function well enough). Babies build from the experiences in which their parents successfully comfort them to being able to comfort themselves. The mouth quickly becomes a source not only of pleasure but also of comfort. As soon as babies can reliably get their fingers in their mouth, often within the first weeks, sucking their thumb is both pleasurable and settles them. If babies feel they are on the point of falling apart, thumb sucking helps them reintegrate, in the way that the teat in the mouth would or using a dummy. If they feel themselves to be agentive, they internalize their parents' soothing. Gradually babies recognize that calming themselves is under their own control and that they are not so dependent on other people for this, which adds to their sense of being effective.

A 7-week-old baby had a number of ways of self-soothing such as gazing at the bath taps or the lights or table legs and falling rapidly asleep. An 8-week-old boy who tried to scream turned his cry into a lyrical crying noise and made a number of sounds that he explored in turn. Each time he created a new sound he was pleased with it and gave a big smile. His playful monologues became part of his contemplation of his self. A 3-month-old girl often joined her hands together as if she was discovering herself. It became a more coordinated and satisfying movement, and she seemed to feel she could look after herself with it.

## Smiling

Parents read their babies' smiles in the first two months as indicating that they are developing their own individual self. Babies rapidly develop in the first few months a repertoire of smiles that convey what they feel about the person they are with. They have a social smile, which they may give anyone, and a full-beam smile—the lighthouse or "dynamite" one—which is reserved for their parents and other children who amuse them.

A 4-month-old baby assessed newcomers with mature seriousness, slowly breaking into a radiant smile and a chuckle, as though after he recognized them he was having a conversation. Seven-month-old babies can give cheeky smiles. If they are alarmed about something, but feel that they should smile or that it would be safer to smile, they may do so warily. Occasionally parents may have a sense that a baby is smiling in an even more brilliant way than the full-beam smile, as though the baby feels that he is in a situation in which he needs to be especially disarming. Or a smile may seem like the baby being a "good" baby and compliant rather than fully expressing his feelings, or the smile might crumple quickly. These indicators are helpful for parents to reflect on what in the situation at that moment is worrying their baby.

## The psychosomatic body

As babies start discriminating between what is physical and what is emotional, and their capacity to express feelings develops, their use of their bodies to convey emotional distress lessens. A 4-month-old baby's distress was evident when her mother, in desperation to supplement the feed, tried while breastfeeding to insert a thin tube over her own shoulder and into the baby's mouth. The baby, an otherwise healthy baby, felt there was something tricky happening, and her lips and mouth began turning blue.

Babies "read" the information from other people's actions and touch very well, whether the touch is tender, or confident, or the opposite. As feelings are experienced in the mind and the body at the same time, a dialogue of feelings in the baby's first "language" takes place when a baby is held.

A 2-month-old boy was referred for failing to thrive. In the first visit, the clinician held the floppy baby while he talked to his mother and grandmother and learnt that the grandmother's baby son had died at birth thirty years earlier. The family's unresolved grief and anxiety seemed to be contributing to this baby's difficulties in thriving. At the same time as talking to the mother and grandmother, the clinician talked to the baby, who became more erect, smiled at his mother for the first time, and vocalized vigorously to her. Emotionally as well as physically by touch, the clinician had communicated both receptivity to the baby's tremulous fear as well as safety.[1]

## Self-consciousness

A kind of shy self-consciousness can be seen in babies from about 6 weeks, when they give a coy smile and their arm curves up over their face to hide it: the baby has an awareness of the self as different from the other person and momentarily in the interaction has felt overwhelmed. From 2 months onwards, they are beginning to become aware of, or conscious of, themselves. As babies want intensely to relate to other people who are important to them, they could well be aware when they had not got it right in an interaction.

By about 3 months, babies become so much more interested in the outside world that the early sense of communion, particularly with their mother, is replaced by their actively turning away to explore a world of other people and objects. Their sense of self is more developed and might be threatened if they felt that they merged too often with their mother. A 12-week-old boy looked excitedly at a female visitor and wiggled, but when she picked him up he immediately turned to the windows. She turned him to see his face, and he smiled at her but then looked away again, bashfully.

From 4 months onwards, babies' coyness when looking at their parents, other babies, and in a mirror has more shades of meaning. When the observer of a 6-month-old girl arrived, the baby smiled and put her head down on her arm coyly and then held out her right hand. The coyness suggested the sudden reaction of a child who has had a fantasy and holding her hand out was a communicative gesture. While she did not want to be picked up, as that was her mother's domain, she wanted to make an arms-length connection with the observer.

## Mapping and enjoying the body

Babies learn about a succession of bodily pleasures, starting with being kissed and caressed. They respond so well to being touched and stroked that premature babies who are massaged while they are still in hospital thrive physically and emotionally.

Babies map where they end and the rest of the world begins. Their mouths are a superb way of exploring new objects, as their experiences of sucking have made them very sensitive instruments of exploration. They discover their hands, as if they are new objects floating in front of them, and their toes at the end of their legs. Sometimes they pat their legs all the way from their toes to where their legs join their body. A 4-week-old boy conveyed his developing sense of self as he focused on his different limbs. With his left leg he made rhythmic bike-riding movements, while his right leg stayed bent and open. Sometimes he stretched out his right leg so it was straighter and flexed his left leg. At times he opened his right hand with the fingers in a spider shape or touched his clothes. When he became unhappy, he moved his open hand more vigorously, held his hands together, and settled.

By 4 months of age or earlier, babies are aware of the sounds they make. A 10-week-old boy experimented with joining up the cry sound with the crying expression. He opened his mouth wide as if he was crying but no sound came out. He paused, relaxed all his face muscles, looked surprised, but realized that he was all right. He moved different parts of his face, opened his mouth wide and closed it, squinted his eyes and relaxed them, tightened up his nose and relaxed it, and in the pauses smiled to himself. He was playing and was pleased at his mastery. Then, with his face muscles relaxed, he started to cry as if experimenting with sound. After a short while, he integrated the crying noises and the crying facial expression and started and stopped the crying, as if playing a game, because there were pauses when he smiled with pleasure at what he had created.

We need to be open to the possible richness of the baby's experience. For example, when we watch a baby determinedly tugging off his sock, we may think no further about this movement. But if we watch him closely we may pick up clues about what he is thinking—could he be imagining that it is another skin that he needs to explore?

Babies become entranced with games such as having raspberries blown on their tummies or other games with their hands and arms. Some babies contain their excitement with rhythmical gestures; with others, their limbs quiver ecstatically. Another source of pleasure is their appreciation of musical play, and 6-month-old babies can discriminate features of tempo, rhythm, melody, and key.[2] A 7-month-old girl was heard singing/humming the first few bars of the nursery rhyme, "Old McDonald's Farm".

Pleasurable thumb sucking contributes to an ongoing sense of well-being and self-esteem. At some point in the first year, babies usually discover their genitals and, if they have the opportunity, will explore them with pleasure, touching and rubbing them. As with thumb sucking, masturbation takes its place as part of the normal unfolding developmental sequence of enjoying one's own body. The developing self becomes an enjoyable one. Finding the genitals and deriving pleasure from them contributes to the development of a gendered sense of self.

Thumb sucking only becomes problematic if it becomes anxiety-driven. Parents can recognize that this is happening when there is immediate recourse to such activity when babies are anxious, rather than being able to try other things that have soothed and settled them in the past. Such activity takes on a desperate, driven quality, so that any pleasure in it is overridden, and when it fails to provide a solution to what the babies are worried about, the cycle starts again.

## Differentiating self from other

Babies' face-processing system develops extremely fast in the first year of life. They can recognize their mother's face from the others around them within minutes of birth, and in a matter of hours they start to differentiate other adults' faces. Very quickly babies integrate the different pictures they have of their parents—leaning over them, turning away, laughing—to realize they are all of the same person. By the age of 6 months, babies can not only pick out familiar faces from a crowd of people, but also, as a test showed, can even distinguish one monkey from another (6-month-olds outperformed adults in this latter test!).

From about age 5 months, if not earlier, some of the baby's actions are aimed at differentiating their mother from themselves. Babies as young as 3 weeks have been described as lovingly stroking their mother's face, but from about 5 months onwards they are much more purposeful in exploring their own and their parents' faces, clothes, and body, and they check from their mother to another person and back again. Sometimes they pull away from her in order to make these observations. Several actions are typical in the next three to four months.[3] When babies touch their mother's nose and she responds, "Where's your nose?" they learn about her as another person for whom they have feelings. These actions are primarily explorative rather than aggressive. When babies touch their fingers with their own fingers, it feels different from being touched by another person. Touching their mother feels different from touching themselves. From this they learn that a double touch always signifies themselves; a single touch always means another person. In the peek-a-boo game, babies consolidate their learning about the disappearance of their parents, that they leave and return. In the "customs' inspection", they examine objects and their mothers smile at them, name the object, and respond, making the experience mutually pleasurable. When held, babies may peer out like a bird craning, no longer limp in their mother's arms the way they were when as very young babies they and their mother looked as one. Their reaching-away creates the sensation of being separate from the other person.

By about 7 months, babies may not like it if, for example, their mother changes the colour of her hair or its style. It is not that they do not know her, but in some ways they prefer the familiarity.


## Temperament

A baby's "temperament"[4] comprises characteristic ways of responding emotionally and behaviourally to the environment. Two main clusters are those of the "easy" child and the "slow-to-warm" child, and there is a small number of children with a "difficult" temperament. Temperament has constitutional origins and affects how babies' experience their self. Individual differences help illuminate why some babies experience developmental phases smoothly and others do not.

The "fit" between temperamentally sensitive babies or less reactive babies and their parents also comes into play. Caring for an easy baby may be blissfully straightforward. Babies who are generous and compassionate are easy to parent. Secure babies are more likely to be outgoing. Children who are brave or passionate, and seek out challenges, may stretch their parents without overstraining their resources. While some parents may find it temperamentally easier to deal with a very active baby or a slightly passive one, parents and babies can usually make changes to meet each other's expectations more enjoyably. When babies are slow-to-warm and timid, and their parents had hoped for them to be outgoing, their parents can often coax them into being more confident and not needing to control so much as a way of coping with their anxiety.

These descriptions of temperament are global ones, and it is more helpful to get to know the individual qualities and responses of each baby. Babies vary about how much they like or dislike the introduction of ideas that are not their own, as well as in their capacity to tolerate another person's involvement with them. Some easy babies seem satisfied with very little input, but even an easy, settled baby may become unsettled when making the transition from hospital to home. Some babies prefer routines, whereas others are not the least dependent on them. Sometimes babies get described early on as greedy. Some babies seem driven by anxiety so they need to bolt their food as if they felt starved of love and attention, whereas other babies seem to have a larger-than-usual appetite for life that might be helpful later on. Ways to think about this include considering whether babies are able to enjoy any of the feed, to pause and share experiences with their mother, as well as what else is happening in their lives and whether they seem generally happy, relaxed, and outgoing.

Babies need their parents' thinking not to foreclose too soon and opt for a quick answer. When parents are faced with some hard-to-read behaviour in their new baby, their capacity to think without rushing into activity or dismissing the behaviour helps them to "hold" their baby until they understand it. Some babies get very upset if they have to wait a second too long for a feed. If they are sobbing in grief, they might take the breast immediately, whereas other babies, if they are angry, have to be settled before they will take the breast. In their upset state, they no longer register that the breast is there to feed from. For them, the world has become a bad, horrible place when the feed does not arrive quickly enough; they may be cross about having to wait, and their sense of being in charge is challenged.

Children with a difficult temperament may need considerable help in their struggle not just to master their endowment but also to enjoy it. For some, their experiences are so intense they are almost dysregulated, which makes the task of achieving a balance as part of becoming emotionally separate particularly hard. Some babies find it hard to give up a grudge, holding onto it for weeks. Others find it hard to share, although any young child who feels deprived envies what he is missing, whether it is attention or love. It is sometimes difficult for parents to understand why some children spoil good experiences and to see the anxiety that usually lies behind such behaviour.

Such traits may strain new parents. But it seems more helpful for parents for other people not to dismiss their baby's struggles as his having a difficult temperament. If the difficulty is seen as being entirely in the baby this may leave the parents feeling that there is nothing they can do, whereas parents have an enormous role here in helping their child enjoy his life and in positively influencing his development.

If the parents of babies with a difficult temperament can be supportive, a good outcome is likely. Some of the positive qualities such a child may possess are liveliness, inquisitiveness and determination, a will to succeed, and the confidence and courage to believe in himself and to take risks. If these qualities can be nurtured, such children will do better than if they mainly meet with punishment; if they are bright, they may, for example, end up a leader.

## Self-esteem

Babies' self-esteem grows according to the love and enjoyment they feel they receive. Being under the luminous gaze of a parent or another important person very vividly gives a baby a sense of being loved and valued. As a baby comes to feel separate from his mother, he starts to love himself in the way he feels she loves him.

Being observed for an hour a week by an interested observer usually contributes to a baby's self-esteem. A 6-month-old baby enjoyed being watched by her observer and often looked round to check that she was observing. When the baby's sister jealously squeezed her leg, the baby did not cry. She seemed to feel, "I've got this woman here for me, so I don't mind. She's holding me, so if someone pinches my leg that's all right. I've got this good experience, so I can tolerate what happens."

## Complex relational feelings

Babies express not only feelings such as interest, joy, distress, disgust, and surprise very early, but also blended feelings. From the second month onwards, babies are capable of complex relational feelings. When people say admiringly to them about how pretty they look or how great they are, their chest puffs up and their response is unmistakably one of feeling happy and appropriately proud of themselves and their achievements. When babies feel that they have successfully captured another person's attention and approval, they have a developmentally appropriate sense of pride. Pride and feeling happy with oneself become important ways of feeling about the self, as conversely may shame and embarrassment.

Colwyn Trevarthen, most of whose life's work has been spent researching and videoing babies, wrote that by 6 months old they are, "adventurous, theatrical, curious, quick to shift attentions and aware of their 'image' as actors in others' eyes and ears. . . . [They] also show off, sulk, challenge, mock, protest, flirt and show a proud indulgent love for a good act of friendship, and shame when their efforts to share are rebuffed or misconstrued."[5] By about 7 months of age, babies try to draw attention to themselves by showing off to get praise and clowning to evoke laughter. A 7-month-old was described as bossy in getting her point across. The following example gives an idea of the complexity of a 5¼-month-old girl's relationship with her observer, whom she liked.

When the observer arrived, the baby gave her a big grin, wiggling on her back with pleasure. She then looked at her mother and cried, and her eyes said, "Pick me up." The observer felt that there was more knowing in the baby's eyes every time. After being fed some solids, she cried in pain and stared at the observer fairly steadily, and she had done this before when she could not be settled. What she communicated in her eyes was, "I don't know what's happening to me, am I going to be all right? Don't go away!" The observer thought that the baby might be pleading with her to help her and was looking for what she felt in the observer's face and that her gaze communicated, "The way you look at me is different". When her mother did things with her, she continued to look at the observer. A baby knows that the observer watches her continually, so that the observer's face becomes a fascinating screen for the baby to see what is reflected there.

Other complex feelings appear on the scene such as jealousy and the wish to exclude, alongside the pleasure in reaching out to other people. Babies may show interest in relating to other babies, possessiveness in wanting to keep their attention, and negativity about sharing it (see also chapter 10).

Towards the end of the first year, babies' actions may have a wilfulness to them, which is about developing their autonomy. An onlooker may respond to these actions as amusing or may welcome the protest in them. A 12-month-old boy kept standing up at the top of the slide despite his mother saying "no" clearly, and he hugely enjoyed his show of disobedience, in which he was partly teasing her.

## Hurt and shame

Some babies recover quickly from hurts to the body; others take longer, as though their sense of pride in themselves is injured. Quite early, babies can look hurt and disappointed. A 7-week-old girl gave her mother a very hurt look when she was taken off the breast before she was ready. A 3-month-old girl looked disappointed when she lost her mother's attention, turned away, and refused to engage, even when her mother turned her round, until she was sure she had her mother's attention.

From 2 months onwards, babies can have reactions of shame if they feel that they cannot entrance their parents and feel misunderstood or disliked. They respond with a sad avoidance that looks like distressed embarrassment or shame. Many babies look ashamed if they cannot make themselves understood to a stranger or the stranger is not sympathetic to them, and they avoid eye contact if they do not want people to see their sense of shame. Some babies get so dejected at separations that their responses look as though they are rejecting their parents, because they feel so hurt and are protecting themselves.

Babies are extremely sensitive to sarcasm. A 10-week-old baby girl heard it in her mother's voice after they had been smiling and chatting and suddenly her mother said fairly softly but with a bitter touch, "You think you're very clever". The baby turned away from her immediately, all the sunniness gone. Her mother tried to pursue the game, but the baby refused to meet her eyes and was sad. In contrast, a 3½-month-old boy became increasingly aware that he had to wait while his mother attended to everyone else. When she told him to say "hello" to a visitor, he took a furtive look at her, smiled in an embarrassed way, as if he was caught out not doing something right and needed to be polite, and looked away. He repeated this three times. Even though he was a much-loved baby, he seemed to feel ashamed.[6] It seemed likely that his mother attending to everyone else before him had contributed to his feeling not worthy of attention and beginning to feel ashamed of himself.

Identifying how babies could feel that they had not entranced their parents could point the way towards remedying this through the time and attention that parents give their babies, the praise they give them, and the tone of voice in which they speak to them. It is important to help babies with these feelings, as feeling ashamed may lie at the root of a number of later difficulties; it may increase feelings of envy and make it shameful to ask for help.

## Anxiety and fantasying

Babies have many anxieties—some realistically based, as babies are relatively unprotected, and other anxieties stemming more from their imagination. As babies are so little, their fears seem much bigger to them. If we lie on the floor, we immediately have a different perspective of how huge things seem!

It helps to think imaginatively about the thoughts, feelings, and fantasies that babies could have. When at the end of a breastfeed a baby sucks on an empty breast, the nipple between their gums may feel hard and ungiving to them, as if it might even retaliate. Some of the angry feelings that babies experience may contribute to their being unable to feed, settle, or thrive. If they are very angry with their parents and have images of destructiveness, they may develop a terror of what they fear they may do to their parents or they fear may be done back to them in turn. Some of the primitive images that children have towards others—of wanting to bite, chew them up, and spit them out—begin at this time. When parents understand that their baby is cross about something, they can safely play it out with them—for example, talking about a toy crocodile's cross, bitey feelings.

## Anger and ambivalence

Babies' anger in the first year seems so often stimulated by their anxiety or frustration or tiredness that it has a self-protective function. When babies fail to accomplish their goals, which include movement and social interaction, this generates anger. Many babies feel angry if they have to wait too long when they are hungry or if they feel the freedom of movement of their arms or legs is restrained. Two-months-old babies whose wrists were connected to a mobile hanging above their cot looked joyful when they discovered that their arm movements made the mobile move, and they were angry when their wrists and the mobile were disconnected. Their reactive aggressive outbursts are short-lived, especially when the impingement on them stops.

A 5-week-old baby made shouting and growling noises, getting angry and irritated when his mother was out of the room. His eyebrows were heavily knitted, and his mouth opened very wide when he complained. When she returned, his lip dropped and he started to cry. He looked angry at her and tried to communicate he was upset that she had left him. Another baby was described as making the direction of his gaze go into the back of his head when he was angry.

An observer, who had visited a 2½-month-old girl weekly, thought that she demonstrated a *passive–aggressive response*. She had been crying for her mother, who was in another room, and throughout her absence watched in the direction in which

she could hear her mother. When, however, her mother returned, the baby seemed to studiously avoid any acknowledg-
ment that she was happy to see her mother.

The struggle that babies have with their ambivalent feelings
becomes clearer towards the middle of the year. A 6-month-old
girl arched her back as if trying to get away from her mother.
She seemed to be ambivalent about whom she wanted to be
with, wanting to be with whomever she was not. She seemed to
be saying, "Yes, that looks great but when it gets too close, I
want my distance again." Biting or chewing the breast is another way of expressing the ambivalence.

Babies sometimes use moments of anger to define and
protect their sense of self against inroads. A baby's *protest*, in
this light, is a basis of autonomy of their developing self. But
when babies become troubled by their angry feelings towards
their parents, they need to feel that these have been resolved
or they may be too troubled to fall asleep easily. They need to
feel that their parents can survive their anger. If babies fail to
build up a sense that the world is not an angry place but, rather,
is one in which it is safe to fall asleep, their sleep is likely to
suffer.

Occasionally babies do not have the experience of having
their wishes frustrated a little before being eventually met,
because their parents pre-empt this experience. Parents may
feel that to be good parents they should meet all their babies'
needs without them even knowing that they feel them. For
some babies, this experience can contribute to them feeling
angry about lacking a space for their own experiencing and
autonomy. For most babies, their parents trying to do everything they want usually makes them more insecure, because
there is no boundary and no conviction that the parents are in
control and can protect them.

## What babies need from their parents

Babies need their parents' physical holding and caring for them to help them learn to self-soothe and self-regulate. But they also need their parents' emotional holding-in-mind so that they can internalize that as part of their own way of looking after themselves. To really think about a baby means to feel your way into what that baby is thinking.

Parents who regulate well for themselves provide a model for their baby to use. When parents feel that it is all too much, their capacity to leave their babies for a ten-minute coffee break—provided, of course, that the baby is not unwell or hurt—shows the baby that they can all survive. Similarly when babies squish up their food at meal times or get into messy play, the capacity to temporarily turn a blind eye helps to lessen the number of preventable battles and also helps babies on their path to learning to self-regulate.

## Holding babies' memories

As part of the scaffolding that parents provide, babies need them to hold memories for them. By 5 months, babies can remember for several weeks an object seen for only a few minutes, and much of their memory is concerned with the minutiae of everyday life—the pointing out, reminding, and replaying.

Sometimes parents hold memories that make children understandable to themselves and to others. While explicit memories of the first year are usually not recoverable, some may be remembered. Susan Coates described how, when she put her 7-month-old nephew to bed and he kicked her, she kissed his feet and made a game out of it. They never had the same experience together again. When he was 2 years old his grandfather tickled his feet, and the boy said, "Susan, feet".[7] He had a memory that felt like, "I was there and it happened to me."

Babies from about 6 months onwards can recognize themselves in photos, showing a different kind of delight in recognizing themselves from recognizing other people.

## Conclusion

As the year goes on, babies have a more coherent sense both of themselves as a baby with feelings and memories over time and of other people as different and with their own feelings and existence. The feelings, thoughts, and intentions known about and shared between them and others also increase their sense of self, as we will see in chapter 5.

# 5

## a baby's empathic self

Babies have been described as wise and knowing. Is this far-fetched, or is it based on a solid knowledge of babies? Empathizing is the natural way to understand a person and occurs when feelings are triggered by another person's feelings. Understanding the feelings of other people and sharing subjective experiences takes place very early. A mirroring system for matching expressive states between people is active in the brain of a 2-month-old baby[1] and provides a neurobiological basis for intersubjectivity or empathy in its widest sense, so that one person can share the feelings and thoughts of another person. Intersubjective communication helps to build an important aspect of the self.

From 7 months, if not earlier, babies begin social referencing—checking their parent's emotional expressions to find signals of safety or danger as they explore.[2] They can communicate that they want their parents to look where they are looking, so the parents will see how exciting it is and share their babies' pleasure.

## Developing expectancies

The capacity to understand other people's feelings and be empathic with them develops throughout this period. Babies convey to other people that they are trying to understand what that person is thinking and feeling. Their attunement to other small children is easy to see: they are pleased and excited about being around them and sad and low-keyed if another child is quiet.

From very early on, babies are acutely sensitive to the feelings of those caring for them and rely on their intuitive interpretations of people. They blossom in their parents' serenity and register acutely their feelings. A 6-week-old girl who was exhausted did not settle in her mother's arms when they were at a party, but the moment an older woman held her she fell asleep, despite not knowing this woman. What was communicated to the baby was a calmness that her own mother at that moment did not have.

Babies quickly build up expectations about how adults act, and they recognize patterns in what other people do. By 6 weeks of age, if their mothers switch attention from them to take a phone call, the babies indicate that this is expectable. If, however, mothers who had interacted in a lively way with their babies then hold an unresponsive face for up to two minutes, babies become derailed by this. They become unhappy and distressed, although they recover quickly when their mother starts talking and playing with them as she did before. Already at this age they have an expectation of the turn-taking that happens in ordinary playful exchanges and that this has been violated when their mother slips out of role.

Babies generalize from repeated sequences to build expectations. If an observer who visits weekly does not have physical contact with the baby and then varies this, the baby can react strongly. One 6-month-old baby had not previously been anxious about occasional contact with her observer, but when she wanted the observer to push her in her swing, she found it frightening when the observer did so. It was as though she had broken an invisible barrier, which was that "Only Mummy is supposed to do this."

## Babies need their parents' thinking mind

Babies need to know they are in their parents' mind. For their minds to grow to the fullest potential, they need their parents to relate to them with understanding and pleasure. Across cultures, mothers talk to their own and other babies in a sing-song "motherese", in which their voices rise as much as two octaves. Babies turn to these sounds more than to the tones adults might use to each other, and their heart rate steadies. Fathers' voices rise too, though not as much. A mother, when she is talking to her baby, takes *turns*—usually without realizing it—to interact with the baby in a synchronized way. A mother will say something, pause, and wait until her baby vocalizes and then she responds, and this can continue for quite some time, usually until the baby tires of it.

When a baby is at the centre of his parents' loving thoughtfulness or reverie,[3] the parents' intuitive feelings allow them to be in touch at a deep level, accessing parts of themselves from the time when they were babies. Babies long to feel that their parents are sufficiently *attuned* to their feelings, intuitively knowing and understanding them so that they can accept them and reflect this back. Attunement is essentially playful. Babies may bang a toy, and their mothers clap or pat them in time, not copying but in tune with the feelings infusing what they are doing. Parents tap into the baby's rhythms of activity, vocalization, or physical expression, and their reflecting-back their baby's self-generated rhythms strengthens a basic part of their baby's sense of self. When babies know that their parents know what they are feeling, they feel "met" by them. When parents feel their way into their baby's mind it is a slipping into their mind. This "feeling felt" is of crucial importance for babies to develop a sense that they are understandable to themselves. This early experience of parents attuning to their baby contributes to later feelings that the baby has of being at one with another person. Babies whose parents are attuned, responsive, and sensitive are likely to be securely attached.

## The language of the eyes

The language of the eyes can be seen in babies from the earliest weeks, and the mother's gaze seems to hold a baby together more than feeling the nipple in the mouth. A 3-month-old baby can look beseechingly at his parents when he wants to be picked up rather than given something to play with. From 4 months onwards, a baby's sense of confusion around the eyes or even apparent disinterest signals anxiety in the presence of something unpredictable.

A mother's emotionally expressive face is the most powerful visual stimulus for her baby, and her baby's gazing at her entrains her gaze. More poetically, gaze has been described as mothers *mirroring* for their babies what they see of them. This mutual gazing is the most intense form of interpersonal communication. One mother said: "It melts your heart and your brain is addicted for the rest of your life." The fovea (the pit in the retina for focusing images) of a mother's eyes increases fivefold as she gazes at her baby, so that what is referred to in everyday language as the sparkle in a mother's eye might literally be a flash or a sparkle.[4] For the baby, visual interactions release endogenous opiates. Babies thrive when they get their parents' attention. For secure attachment it is essential for them to feel at the centre of their parents' attention enough of the time. Securely attached children feel they have had a "wrappedness of attention"[5] so that they could find their feelings in a mirroring mother.

Let us return to the idea that babies need their parent's mind for optimum development. Babies need to feel that they are securely held, not only physically but also emotionally in their parents' mind. They need to feel that their parents can tolerate and manage their distress and other feelings. The ideal way is for parents to be able, by thinking about these, to transform what may feel to their baby to be unbearable anxiety into something that becomes more manageable. Parents so often say to their baby when soothing him, "It's all right, you're not going to die": they have intuited just how anxious their baby feels, because they too have felt it. Many parents know what their babies are feeling because they feel it almost instantly. Communicating to another person so that they know a baby's feeling, through crying and facial and bodily gestures, is the only way a baby can communicate. A parent transforming the feeling in a thoughtful way provides holding and *containment*[6] of a baby's feelings.

The very precise turntaking by mother and baby from the beginning forms a system, even if it is an asymmetrical one. It is an ever-changing and therefore *dynamic system*. When parents "lend" their babies their capacities, they put at their disposal their understanding, pleasure, and encouragement. Babies are therefore capable of doing much more than they would otherwise have been able to on their own. This acts as a s*caffolding* so that babies can function at a higher level. With this support, they are propelled towards the next level of development and can function there.

Suppose babies feel something quite strongly, such as anxiety. If babies feel that their parents understand the feeling, without pretending to have it, and that at the same time they are not overwhelmed by it, this helps babies to develop the capacity to master it, as well as the capacity for pretend play and symbolizing experience.

When parents hold their babies in mind, it helps them differentiate their representations of themselves and other people. Let me explain. When parents can be thoughtful, babies experience their parents' responses as appropriate to what they need at that moment. The parents' responses are neither too rigid nor slapdash and stretch the babies appropriately, nudging them to take the next step by very slightly misattuning and helping them find a response. The responses confirm to the babies the kind of person that they feel themselves to be and that they are different from their parents, who act in ways that are expectable.

## Intersubjective communication of feelings

Often around age 7 months, babies sense that they have an internal subjective life and that others do too. Babies can sense when an empathic process bridging two minds has been created. They show a desire for intimacy, to know and be known in mutually revealing subjective experience. The process involves learning that their subjective life—their thoughts and their feelings—can be shared with another person. They become more interested in the mental states that give rise to actions.

A 7½-month-old boy communicated several related feelings very clearly. He smiled excitedly when his observer said hello then coyly tucked his head down and looked again at her. She felt that the way he invited her in was different. The mother, who felt that the boy's relationship with her herself had also changed, particularly around breastfeeding, said, "He just wants to sit and play with my nipple now. Look how he touches my body all over." He breastfed in a different way, as though he was controlling the feed himself. He seemed to know he had the exclusive attention of two women. He sat up immediately after the feed, satisfied, and looked at the observer as though saying, "I'm here, and this is where I want to be". When his brother blocked his gaze at his mother, he became quite agitated and distressed: he was staking a claim on his mother in a new way—"I want to be with you."

Nine-month-old babies enjoy sharing a secret with adults whom they know well, and they can behave in a conspiratorial way that is different from how they are with their parents. Everyone has a necessary *private* part of the self, and these babies are beginning to develop this. A 5-month-old baby seemed to understand when her observer signalled to her to be quiet as her mother did not want the baby to be disturbed. The baby was amused but kept quiet. When the observer tried to melt into the background, putting the bars of the cot between her and the baby, the baby was delighted to move so that her eyes appeared either side of the cot bars several times, finding her observer.

This example shows the bi-directional flow of emotional communication between a clinician and an 11-month-old boy who had refused to be weaned from the breast. The boy accurately read the communication in the clinician's actions.[7] When the boy's mother started to wean him, he refused the bottle and all food and would not let her hold him. He hit her, pulled her hair, screamed, threw things at her, and did not accept her overtures. She was distraught about his distress. The clinician commented, "He's really angry with you." The boy picked up a soft ball and flung it, yelling, at his mother and then clenched his lips. The clinician caught the ball and, attuning to his anger, threw the ball back to the foot of the cot. He was instantly engaged, recognized the communication, smiled, and returned the ball for the clinician to throw again. It gradually became a quieter catching game, which he let his mother join in. The meaning to him of the loss of the breast had contributed to her difficulties in thinking. The clinician intuitively knew that in play his rage at feeling deprived by his mother and the breast could be accepted. With his next feed, his anger had gone, the good relationship had returned, and he could accept food from his mother. She became less tearful and more confident and initiated a successful, caring weaning.

## Identification with others

Identification is a developmental process that helps build up the sense of self. When babies copy adults, they are trying out identifications that may become more enduring. Different strands of identification come from ways of being with someone and ways of being active like someone. Babies who, for the first three months of their life, enjoy a communion with their mother have as part of them a way of just being. Then, as they reach out to the world and want to be like people who do things, they have an active strand to their personality.[8] These ideas are partly illustrated in the comments of the observer of a 5-month-old boy. She said that when he looked at her, she felt very anxious because the look was about what relationships are about. This was because what the baby did was to "be"—he did not "do", the way that children and adults learn to keep themselves busy. She felt the experience with him went back to something fundamental about people being together that babies have to grapple with.

Babies may copy what they see their parents doing: going to work like Daddy, washing dishes like Mummy. Babies also identify with feelings that animals have. A 5-month-old girl froze when she saw a very scared baby rabbit.

## Teasing

When babies tease another person, they know what that person expects them to do and that if they do not do what is expected, there will be a reaction from the other person. Often from 5 months onwards babies hold out a toy or some food to another person and then withdraw their hand, and this can become a teasing game. The baby knows what the other person expects and that the person may mind or be disappointed not to get what he or she had expected. This quickly becomes amusing for the baby who repeats it, especially if the adult's reaction also becomes one of increasing amusement. This kind of teasing is playful. It is more elaborate than showing off and, in the older baby, may be closer to trying to trick the parent to do or get what the baby wants, such as little sorties towards something that the parent does not want the baby to touch. That the baby, when discovered, grins rather than looking serious usually indicates what the baby is trying to do.

## Gender differences in empathizing

Sex differences develop throughout the first year. Perhaps because babies of about 6 months of age have more awareness of their sense of self, they can differentiate at this age the gender of another baby. While the following findings about sex differences may not hold for all boys and all girls, they describe a majority of children. Twelve-month-old girls look at their mother's face significantly more often than boys do. When given a choice of films of a face or cars to watch, boys look longer at the cars and girls look longer at the face. Boys continue to develop their capacities to understand systems, while girls from 12 months onwards "respond more empathically to the distress of other people, showing greater concern for others through more sad looks, sympathetic vocalizations and comforting behaviour".[9]

## The achievements of the self

It needs to be stressed that all babies want to make sense of their lives, to understand themselves, as much as they can, given that they are in the process of developing the internal structures to do so. By the end of the first year, if babies' development has gone well enough, this gives them a good foundation for understanding themselves. They have a sense of their own self with their feelings, their body, and the experiences they have had. They understand something about other people having minds whom they can relate to and influence, and they have a confident expectation that they are likable and that their needs will be met.

To some extent it does not matter if their parents do not always read them absolutely correctly. If babies have to find ways to get their parents to re-engage with them, and they learn what works and what does not, this is beneficial for developing a sense of confidence and security. When babies are able to cycle back quickly from negative feeling states to positive ones, they are usually resilient babies.

## Capacity to play alone

A parallel achievement is a baby's capacity to play alone in the presence of another person.[10] When babies are securely established as a person and enjoy their own company, they are able to play alone in a contented and self-sustaining way. A mother helps her baby to concentrate on the self-exploration that is the essence of solitary play and to forget her. This is the opposite of being lonely. A baby has arrived at a sense of confidence in emotional communication with others. For a constant "true" sense of self, a baby needs to be able to play alone.

## Expressing feelings

Parents sometimes try to protect their baby from seeing their feelings of grief or anger. However, it seems preferable rather than unhelpful for babies to see these feelings authentically expressed rather than hidden away or denied. Part of the brain helps to work out when other people are relating in an authentic way or not, so that if feelings are masked, babies may end up feeling confused. Babies seem to respond with confusion—sometimes almost with collapse—to the scrambled message that they receive rather than focusing on the parents' wish for them to not be hurt or overwhelmed.

> The very depressed mother of a 7-month-old boy thought that every time he looked at her she had to smile, which led to rather fixed smiling on her part. His body tone was flaccid, he could not sit up, and he looked depressed; he did not look at any one very much and often withdrew into mouthing a toy. Within a week of joining a mother–baby therapy group, he was a transformed child, sitting upright and more engaged with every one; he smiled, moved, and vocalized with pleasure and more clearly communicated what he wanted. What he had experienced in the group were adults and babies relating to him and to his mother in a lively, active, and authentic way, which seemed to have promoted change for him. His mother, seeing the overtures that the other adults and babies made to her and her son, felt they carried the message that there was the hope for change, and she too, like her son, was relieved and more spontaneous.

## Conclusion

Parents feel that their baby's first birthday is an important watershed. Some of their early anxieties about whether their baby will or will not live have lessened. The first birthday marks the enormous development that babies have accomplished within a relatively short space of time. Although there are some gender differences in empathizing, these are less important than the fact that from birth onwards babies are sensing, as part of their journey towards self-knowledge, that other people are feeling and thinking in a way that can be knowable to them.

## part II

# THE TASKS FACING
# THE DEVELOPING SELF

"On the seashore of endless worlds, children play."
Rabindranath Tagore[1]

Winnicott used this evocative line capturing the mystery and poetry of the world of babies and young children when describing how babies come to share the cultural life of the environment that they are born into. It is play that has the effect of drawing the child's attention to communication itself.

Parenting is about giving children as much ownership as appropriate of their body and self. It is as though the parents have had guardianship of their babies' capacities and have helped their babies take these over. Part II covers the tasks facing the developing self in the first year.

# 6

## relating to fathers, siblings, and other people

For most babies, a psychologically secure base from which to start exploring the world usually extends from their mother to their father and to other family members such as siblings and grandparents.

## Fathers

Babies quickly become aware of their father and differentiate him from their mother through distinguishing his physical characteristics. They can differentiate their father's voice from the mother's soon after birth and very quickly respond in a preferential way to his voice compared with that of other adults. Fathers usually quickly become important to their babies, who try to draw them in by gesture and vocalization. When the father of a 2-month-old girl went back to work, his daughter cried continuously, missing him.

Babies' attachment relationships with their father cannot be predicted by the type of relationship with their mother but reflects the qualities that the father brings to the relationship. Fathers relate differently to their babies from the way their mothers do and differently again to a son or a daughter.

If babies very much have a love affair with their mother, they may take time to relate at the same depth to their father.

A 9-week-old girl had started to look lovingly particularly at her mother, and her eyes lit up as soon as she sat down. She communicated in an animated and happy way with her mother. When the mother went away and her father sat down, the baby immediately stopped smiling and studied him carefully for a while, but she was not nearly as animated. He held her hand, talked to her, and smiled at her, trying to charm her as much as he could. Her look conveyed that, "You can smile all you like, but I'm still not there with you yet." Her head and arm movements were toned down and she did not find him quite as exciting as her mother, but eventually she smiled at him.

If a baby's primary attachment develops more with the father than with the mother, the baby can relate early on in quite different ways to both parents. A 5-week-old boy whose father usually bathed him noticed the difference when his mother bathed him. He stared at the taps a long time, and when he took his eyes off them he frowned a great deal, and seemed unsure, then showed his anxiety by widening his eyes so that the whites showed above the irises.

The importance that fathers have for their children can be seen in those behaviours in which the baby differentiates between the two parents and shows a preferential looking. The father may become the centre of attraction for the baby, who may be delighted with the time and attention the father spends with him. A 6½-month-old boy kept looking at his father, showing tremendous interest in what he was doing.[1] A 7-month-old girl beamed adoringly with her face and her whole body at her father, and her mother called her "a daddy's girl". Sometimes parents come to feel that their baby is trying to separate them, as, for example, when this 6½-month-old boy systematically turned his head away from his mother with whom he had had a very loving relationship.

Fathers help babies extend their range of feelings. A common example is a father returning at the end of the day and hyping up the atmosphere, playing excitedly and throwing the baby up in the air. Fathers often bring this experience quickly to an end, but the total experience helps their babies extend the range of intensity of feeling and learn to manage the descent more than they can with their mothers. Fathers respond to and shape emerging differences in their children's behaviour. In one study of 12-month-old children, the boys tried to touch forbidden things more often than the girls did, and their fathers reprimanded the boys twice as often as their daughters.[2] The girls seemed to pick up on subtle cues such as their father looking disapproving, and such referencing was enough for many girls to get the message of what was permitted. They looked more frequently to pick up the cues that the parent was giving and were more accurate at decoding them. Boys may miss the cues more often and sometimes only seemed to get the message that they were doing something forbidden when there was an explicit verbal disapproval.

Fathers help their babies to start thinking about differences, and they offer the possibility of alternative identifications to those with the mother. When fathers spend time with their babies individually, the babies' self-confidence and social skills improve. When babies find it difficult to give up a very close relationship with their mothers, their fathers can help them separate. A crucial contribution the father makes is that of being a third person who is in a close relationship with the baby's mother. A baby can then explore feelings about being sometimes included in that relationship and sometimes temporarily excluded from it (see chapter 10).

When fathers are physically absent to any great extent, perhaps because of work or divorce or death, babies yearn for him and try to build up a picture of him in their mind. Mothers help them build up such a picture by talking about him and sharing whatever mementoes they have, such as photos or any of his possessions. If the mothers' relationship with the baby's father is or has been a positive one, this is usually what gets transmitted to the baby. When their mother helps them internalize a positive picture of their father, this contributes to a positive picture of themselves and their relationship with him.

If mothers are depressed, babies often start to show a kind of depressed behaviour with their mothers. If their father is not depressed, babies can have a different way-of-being with their father. He therefore keeps open a more hopeful way-of-being until their mother is no longer weighed down with depressive feelings, and he offers a helpful buffer.

## Siblings

By about age 2 months, babies also have special ways of relating to their older siblings. A sibling may be the only one to persist in getting a tiny baby to smile when other people are too busy. Most babies get considerable pleasure from their siblings. Even 4-week-old babies will tolerate older siblings hurting them, because of the pleasure they get in other ways from them.

The parents' identification may initially be more with the older child, with whom they have had a longer relationship and whose sense of betrayal they may resonate with, or their identification may be more with the defenceless baby. This struggle on the parents' part has to be worked through in the early days, when the baby's cries mean he needs feeding and the older child's cries may mean that she feels left out and in need of an emotional feed. The knowledge that usually siblings stand to gain more from a relationship in which they are helped to manage their jealousy and rivalry seems, at this stage, little compensation to the parents. While older children are given the message that their parents will not allow them to hurt the baby, they need to have their feelings of anger, jealousy, and rivalry accepted as universal, without being condemned for having them. It is helpful if parents can name these feelings for the older child. Often the toddler can voice them by suggesting that the parents return the baby or put the baby in the rubbish bin. These wishes on the older child's part are, in effect, murderous wishes, and babies may shut down as though even very early they know that being invisible is a good protection. Some babies, even by 5 weeks, can look quite anxious when their older brother or sister comes near them.

A baby often has some inkling when older children struggle with wishes to get rid of the new baby. These feelings are very hard for parents to witness and know about, perhaps as they evoke their own painful childhood feelings or guilt about causing the older children distress. It is hard to be in touch with the distress of the older children, who feel that they have been displaced and replaced. A 9½-month-old boy, who had not had another young child visit in his home previously, found the presence of a girl toddler quite a threat, and his mother commented that he was jealous. When the girl became interested in the book her mother was reading to the boy, he interposed his body like a barrier between the book and the girl and then started to cry loudly, with his forefinger in his mouth and his head lowered, and he looked sad and vulnerable.[3] A boy whose brother was born when he was 10 months old dragged a heavy object across the room to attack him with. These babies are showing how they feel they have lost their place with the most precious people in their universe. Some babies seem aware of their mother's withdrawal and preoccupation when she is trying for another baby or is pregnant.

*Twins* relate to each other in a range of ways. If their parents view twins as similar, this may reinforce any tendency they have to being similar. They do better if their parents see them as different. They can have different securities of attachment to each other and to their parents. Some twins find being physically together comforting, cry on separation from each other, and are happy when reunited. A pair of 4-week-old non-identical twins both yawned, stretched, moved their heads, and had the same expressions on their faces at exactly the same moment. If one cried, the other one noticed and moved; they moved their heads to touch one another. The mother of a 6-week-old twin girl thought that she had wriggled over to where her sister had previously been lying in the cot, to look for her.

Sometimes the babies resist twinning, and some are so reactive that their parents feel that they cannot be in same room. A twin 4 months of age can show unmistakable signs of jealousy when excluded from the relationship the other twin has with a parent. A 4-month-old twin hit her sister and twisted her ear and, when she was 7 months old, pulled her sister's dummy out and threw it away. Twins can block each other out of their line of vision. If one twin feels that the other gets the parents' attention, he may be so desperate for it that he yells at the top of his lungs and looks smug when he succeeds in getting it.

## Extended family

Babies very quickly relate differentially to members of the extended family, particularly if the family member has a good relationship with the parents. This is probably easiest to see in the relationships babies have with their grandparents, when they are freed from some of the responsibilities that the parents face. It would make sense from an evolutionary point of view for babies to sense quickly who their next of kin are, if they needed their protection. Babies feel this very quickly, even if relatives do not often see their parents. What gets communicated to babies is their parents' warmth of feeling towards the family member and also, perhaps, a similarity in the way the relative interacts with the baby. Their parents' close friends who are interested in the babies also offer such affiliative relationships.

## Other children

From early infancy, babies are interested in other babies and show pleasure in interacting playfully with them. Babies as young as 2 weeks are fascinated with other babies.[4] As they master a motor or vocal skill, they use it with other babies. Babies who are frequently together in the first two months spend time looking at each other and, from age 3 to 4 months, touching each other. They use imitation to open communication with another baby. From about 6 months onwards they become more actively engaged with each other, smiling in response to coos and vocalizations, and they are as social with other babies as babies six months older than them are. Also, at 6 months of age, babies with their mother will respond to a distressed baby by staring attentively and sometimes leaning forward or touching the other baby. At 7 months, a baby in full cry can suddenly stop crying and be all beaming smiles on catching sight of another baby, such is the attraction of other children.

From around 9 months onwards, babies develop more clearly social behaviours with increasing frequency. A 10-month-old is more interested in looking at a child whom he does not know than one he does know. With both mother and other babies present, a baby directs more looks, touches, and proximity-seeking behaviour to other babies than to his mother. Around this time, babies who know each other interact in a social way, offering and receiving objects to and from one another. These behaviours are important because they maximize the likelihood of feedback and the possibility of sustained encounters. When babies see another person as an active participant, they look at the other person's face when handing over an object; otherwise, they look at the object or the other's hand.[5] Babies who know each other play games with each other, such as peek-a-boo, ball games, and run-and-chase. As babies acquire these behaviours of vocal exchange, offer, approach, and smile, the repertoire for their social encounters is fairly complete. Their awareness of other babies' feelings and empathy for them is evident. If one child cries, others often look anxious or upset.

Activities and games are increasingly elaborated with other babies. They give clues that they miss the other children if they are absent, looking round for them and being low-keyed for a time; they also remember the activities they had shared with them, by initiating the same activity. An 8-month-old girl showed both pleasure and empathy at the arrival of a 7-month-old boy and his mother. He and his mother were both depressed. As soon as she saw him, she expressed her pleasure, wriggling and reaching out, and rolled over towards him and tried to hang onto him. She also expressed her concern about his lack of responsiveness. She continually tried to make contact with him, almost as if she were saying, "Why isn't he responding?" Gradually, enlivened by her, he returned her gaze and perked up.

Babies may show increased ambivalence towards other babies, as ambivalence towards their mothers increases by the end of the first year, but this is not always so.

## Conclusion

We have seen the importance that fathers, brothers and sisters, and other family members have for babies and how rapidly other children become a source of learning and enjoyment to them. How babies learn to separate within their attachment relationships will now be explored.

# 7

# attachment and separation

Throughout evolution, babies have needed to stay close and attached to their carers for safety, so that the process of separation occurs within the envelope of attachment.

## The experience of separation

Babies register separations, even if the separations are very short. A 5-month-old girl, left for two hours for the first time with a motherly babysitter, lowered her eyes for seconds when her mother returned, in a way that her mother had never seen before. She was overcome with feelings, both longing for her absent mother as well as wiping her out in the way that she had felt wiped out. Babies can cope with separations, but it is probably always at some cost. Those who are adaptable and easygoing manage separation best. Separations are easier to deal with when there is some attempt to ensure some kind of continuity with the environment with which they are familiar. For other babies, separation, whenever it happens, may feel as though it has come too soon. What a baby needs to develop is a flexible balance between closeness and separation.

Babies prefer that what they read in their parents' eyes is enjoyment. The next best thing is to read that they will be kept safe. If babies read anything else in their parents' eyes, it acts as a separation or loss. So if their parents are preoccupied and the baby does not feel mirrored there, or there is anxiety in the parents' eyes, to the baby it will feel that there is no safety there.

An adult knows that when another person is not there, it just means that they are absent. Very young babies, however, construe it differently. They have to build up a mental structure to know that other people, particularly their mother, exist even when they are not present. If babies are very distressed in their parent's absence, they may be so overwhelmed that it feels as though the one who is absent is the one causing them pain. That the person is not present to bring any relief may feel as though that person is persecuting them by inflicting the bad state they are in. Babies can then feel that an absent person is a hostile one. As their sense of time means that they cannot hold the picture of the absent parent in their mind for very long, the absent person starts to feel "gone" for ever for the baby. If babies have, at a very early age, experienced anxieties spiralling out of control, they may feel as though it is the end of the world. If they feel they have been left too long with very little understanding and little chance to understand, any internal structures they have built up may crumble under the strain of events that they cannot manage psychologically.

Object constancy—when babies can keep a constant picture of an object in their mind—is easily established by age 9 months or earlier. This can be demonstrated cognitively when an object is hidden in different places, and the baby has to search for it. (Boys before they are a year old search for longer for the object in the first hiding place, but they then catch up with girls' development.) Babies' capacity to keep a picture in their mind of a live person with whom they are intimately connected seems to start much earlier than 9 months, although the younger they are the harder it would be for them to keep the memory of this.

## Secure and insecure attachment

Attachment is the deep emotional bond formed between babies and the adults who look after them. While the attachment relationship is universal, the way that parents and children express it differs in different parts of the world. Babies develop a secure base in relationships through their parents being responsive and attuned. For security and confidence, babies need their parents to respect their experience, recognize their feelings, and keep them in mind. Securely attached children are able to explore the world with pleasure and take comfort when necessary from their parents or carers. Parents communicate to their babies that they are safe by having them at the centre of their attention enough of the time and by entering a dialogue of musicality with them. If by the time babies are 4 months old their conversation with their parents has a rhythmic turn-taking that delights them both, they feel valued and safe and are likely to have a secure attachment by the time they are a year old. The turn-taking provides a kind of auditory safe base for babies to tuck themselves into.

By the end of the first year, children who are securely attached will, if they are separated from a parent, explore the room they are in with interest and then show signs of missing the parent, often crying. On their parent's return, they greet the parent and usually initiate physical contact, and then settle. They expect that their protest will be heard and their distress dealt with, and they are then able to return to play. They are developing the capacity to function autonomously in problem-solving procedures.

Self-esteem and security are closely linked. Securely attached babies not only learn faster but are more popular and develop more stable relationships. When babies have an internal secure base, part of this comes from the reassurance of a sense of self—of knowing who they are. Secure attachment is associated with the resilience to face difficult events. The richer the attachment, the richer the child's later relationships, as well as their capacity to manage strong or distressing feelings.

The attachment status of a baby is usually linked with their parent's own attachment status. It is the quality of parental availability that determines the security of a baby's attachment. A mother's own attachment status when she is pregnant is likely to predict her baby's attachment status when her baby is a year old. Although the formal tests of attachment status begin at age 12 months, the quality of the baby's attachment can be seen earlier. Securely attached parents are likely to have securely attached children. Being securely attached refers to those people with whom the baby feels safe. It does not mean that the baby will never feel anxious or worried. When babies feel anxious or worried, orienting towards their attachment figures is usually sufficient to bring relief from the anxieties.

Parents who were insecurely attached to their own parents are likely to have children with the same difficulties. When babies develop an insecure attachment, they find it difficult to explore comfortably or be easily comforted. Parents who have unresolved traumatic events in their own attachment history are likely to have babies with an attachment that is disorganized, making it difficult in turn for them to find security and comfort.

Revisiting issues of temperament, intuitively it seems there would be an overlap between the three main clusters of temperament and the three main kinds of attachment. Children who are easygoing are likely to be securely attached; children who are slow-to-warm or have a difficult temperament may be insecurely attached. Summing up, babies are likely to have attachment disorders if they have constitutional vulnerabilities and are cared for by parents who have their own emotional vulnerabilities and there is a poor fit between the parents and their baby. A baby who starts life with a regulatory disorder or a temperament that is difficult, and with a low threshold for early activity, may overreact to even moderate stimulation and then become fussy and difficult to console. This makes it difficult for the parents to understand the meaning of their baby's response, whether it is arching away or resisting being cuddled, or waking frequently in the night. If it is hard for them to understand the baby's behaviour, they may respond in such a way that the baby feels overwhelmed or full of pain, which in turn affects the baby's response, and so the difficulties compound.

Many children who are insecurely attached do not easily seek comforting with their parents and carers in nurseries when they are distressed but, rather, avoid it. Their carers, however, find themselves making extra efforts to reach out to make contact with these children. A smaller group of insecurely attached children actively resist in a sometimes confusing and hostile way their carers' efforts to comfort them. This group makes it hard for those carers to respond to them without feeling put out, and this is likely to be so for parents.

Parents who are able to be especially nurturing of a child with a difficult temperament will find that he is securely attached. The first year provides parents with the opportunity to help their babies with the different stages that they need to master so that anxiety does not stand in the way of them developing a confident and joyful response to the world. Like much of development in the first year, attachment patterns are not set in concrete—if things change for the better for the parents of a child with an insecure attachment, the attachment relationship is likely to change as well.

## Sleeping

When babies feel safe, they can fall asleep in a relaxed way. Sleep is, after all, a mini-separation. The individual variation between babies is enormous—some babies begin to sleep though the night extremely early, others take much longer to master this. Early on, babies wake up as often as eight times a night, and they gradually learn to get themselves back to sleep. Co-sleeping with parents, which is statistically the norm around the world, can, in the early weeks, provide a sense of security for the baby, who usually then settles into routines more quickly.[1] A secure baby is less disturbed by anxiety and can sleep more easily whatever the circumstances. Parents and babies have to find out what works for each baby. Some babies need to fuss a little before they drift off into sleep, and if this is interrupted and they are picked up they may get overtired. Neither the parents nor the babies themselves may recognize their cues, and they may not be able to fall asleep easily. Other babies may need more of a routine or a pattern of rituals to help signal that it is time to sleep.

If sleep patterns are disrupted, babies need their parents to help discriminate what the reasons might be—for instance, whether they are having trouble sleeping because they are overtired or frightened. They may be intelligent babies who do not need much sleep, enjoy learning about their environment, and hope that their mother can turn it into a game. As when there are difficulties with feeding, babies can get confused if their parents try too many possible solutions too quickly, one after the other.

It seems more helpful to have the perspective that giving babies what they *need* helps them to manage better. For most babies being held and talked to quietly comforts them, but for some finding what works takes time. Some babies need their parents to time what they say to them, perhaps just after the height of their cry when they are drawing breath again, to catch their attention. If parents have enough faith that their baby and they will work it out together, this usually helps everyone to stay calmer.

Some of the advice given to parents may increase their difficulty in tuning in to what is precipitating their babies' distress and being able to lessen it by picking their babies up and comforting them directly. Sometimes when babies feel that their parents have tried one activity after another to soothe them, this is confusing, frightening, and over-stimulating. When they cry, parents may try to get them to sleep instead of easing their distress first. In their attempts to calm babies, there is often no play time, with babies crying more and the parents trying even harder to get their baby to stop crying. If babies become very distressed, they may no longer know what the reason is for the crying. Their distress becomes distressing. They may cry harder, just as water tends to find old channels to run down.

If babies and their mother have had difficult times together during the day, going to sleep may not be so easy. A mother whose baby is awake in the middle of the night may feel driven to the end of her tether when she feels that no one else comes as close as she does to not wanting the baby. When parents can recognize what their baby needs, they can work out what their baby can realistically cope with. A 1-year-old will cope very differently from a 3-week-old baby. If babies are expected too early to cope with being left to cry in a controlled crying routine, when they are distressed at night the internal structures they have developed may give way under the impact of the crying in the darkness of night.

## Weaning and feeding difficulties

As babies gain more control over feeding, this initially involves a number of hidden separations. Gradually babies lose some of the intimate closeness with their mother and her body, which will in time be compensated by the excitement and competence about increasingly being able to feed themselves. Weaning from breast or bottle is a very important separation from the mother. Weaning may begin at any time in the first year, in stages or completely, and may not be completed before the end of the first year. One mother described her feeling that mothers are there to be left, starting with the baby being outside the womb, followed by weaning. Babies react to weaning in different ways, depending on their personality and gender and the age at which it happens, and therefore it has different meanings to different babies. When weaning goes well, it is a developmental achievement. Some easygoing babies may initiate it themselves out of their own developmental trajectory, drinking less and being ready to engage with the world in an independent, adventurous way. If weaning occurs towards the end of the first year and goes well, babies can keep a memory of their mother's breast as a positive source of comfort for a year or so. Other babies find it hard to relinquish the pleasure and comfort of breastfeeding, using the breast almost as a security blanket and have to be helped to give it up. Babies get confused if they feel that their parents try too many things in quick succession. Some babies yearn for the breast that they feel is denied them, whereas other babies turn completely away as if they wanted nothing more to do with it.

Mothers have a complex task in coping with missing the intimacy of feeding and their feelings about not being needed, as well as simultaneously enjoying their baby's movement forwards. They also need to surmount their feeling that they own their baby's body, a natural feeling from having carried their baby inside and spent so much time in the first year caring for them physically. Mothers may need fathers' support to manage weaning.

Parents may find they have gone to considerable lengths in responding to their baby's eating difficulties, such as the parents of the 1-year-old boy whose favourite perch for eating was a window-ledge overlooking the neighbour's kitchen.[2] The question then is whether the baby is beginning to take over responsibility for feeding or whether it has been left in the mother's province as something to battle over.

When breastfeeding continues throughout the first year, it can have quite varied meanings for the child. Sometimes children ask for the breast almost as if just to prove that they can have it during the day, and it may be a more meaningful feed in the evening, recapturing a little of the early mother–baby intimacy.

When feeding difficulties become prolonged, it is often a combination of babies having a strong will or a difficult temperament and their parents missing their cues so that they are not able to have the kind of sensitivity that helps them manage better. Babies can have powerful associations to food that may make them feel sick, such as fear, anger, or sadness, or the volume of the feed may be too much. Parents need then to help their baby replace fear or aversion with curiosity and playful exploration by encouraging mucking about with food, exploring its appearance, textures, smells, and taste.

## Transitional objects and activities

Most babies from about age 4 months onwards develop an attachment to a particular object, such as a dummy or piece of cloth or a soft toy. This gives them something to hold onto so that they do not feel dropped in space (and out of their mother' mind) as they transition through graded separations. This transitional object stands for both the mother and the baby and is not fully a symbol.[3] They may become fearless explorers—as long as the transitional object accompanies them on all their adventures.

From 5 months onwards, if not earlier, the peek-a-boo game that babies and their parents play is a universal attempt to cope with fears about separation by working them through in play and turning it into something pleasurable. Babies can initiate the game by pulling their clothes up over their head. This working through is similar to how later on children master a difficult experience by playing it out at home.

From about age 6 months onwards, a baby's throwing objects, particularly from a high-chair, can have many meanings, including mastery and the pleasure of a game in which the object is retrieved. The babies may be playing and mastering the disappearance and reappearance of their parents, but in the game they feel themselves to have some control.

The transitional object helps a space between mother and baby to open up—a transitional space, a potential space, on the baby's journey to a new way-of-being—and shows the baby's creative capacity to transform an object into a companion. This space between baby and mother is filled with products of a baby's creative imagination—playing, symbols, and cultural life. In this way feelings about separation can be coped with. This space offers a resting-place from the lifelong task of keeping internal and external reality firmly separate.

## Stranger-anxiety

Stranger-anxiety often occurs around age 8 months, as though babies are now much more in touch with what they might lose if they are separated from their parents. Babies often have a variety of responses to strangers other than anxiety, including curiosity, indifference, responding indiscriminately, and wariness. And babies sometimes develop stranger-anxiety towards people with whom they are familiar, so that one week the baby is all smiles and the next is frightened and distressed. It sometimes looks as though babies feel stranger-anxiety around age 2 or 3 months. This could, however, be a basic anxiety when a face looms in at them and it feels that the intimate space of their body, which is usually appropriately mediated for them by their parents, has been breached.

## Helping with separation

The collaboration that babies need from their parents is similar
to the kind of support a coach gives, helping to draw out the
best from those he or she coaches. Helping a baby learn to cope
is similar. Apart from the obvious reassurance and protection
that parents give their baby, they enter their baby's world by
empathizing with their feelings and conveying that the baby
does not need to be worried.

Even though babies do not have many words in the first year,
their understanding is enormous, so that if parents talk to them
about what will happen if there is a separation, babies usually
cope better. Talking to babies about an impending separation
may feel as though it is over their head, and yet something gets
communicated to them. A baby needs opportunities to start
connecting the words with what happens. A 7-month-old girl
who was very anxious about separations from her mother became much less anxious within days after her mother practised
saying "bye-bye" with her and waving. The mother felt that her
baby understood.[4] Mothers also have to face the fact that the
closeness of the early connection between them changes, and
they must individuate from their babies, too.

## Child care

In considering the effects of child care, much depends on the
type and quality of the placement, the parents' attitudes towards it, and the length of time that babies are looked after.
Some babies gain a lot of stimulation and pleasure from being
in a crèche. But other babies, and their parents, may find the
separation difficult. It is harder to leave babies in care in the
second six months than the first six months, as they are more
aware of what they feel they lose.

When there are changes of caregivers, the feeling of the caregivers' holding the memories of a baby's life is disrupted. Babies may at times experience long periods in day care as being in limbo from the time they arrive there to the time when they leave. When they do not feel that they are in anyone's mind, they can feel dropped. Shorter, more frequent periods of child care may therefore be easier for most babies to cope with than fewer, longer periods.

## Conclusion

Securely attached babies cope appropriately with the anxieties of separation, often creating a transitional object to stand for Mummy–me as they negotiate the gap that opens up between them with separation.

# 8

## thinking

Implicit in much of what has been described up to this point is how a baby thinks. Cognition and feelings, which once were viewed as separate, are now much more considered to be indivisible. It is impossible not to feel something at every moment of our lives, even if it is very much a background feeling and we are not aware of it. How we feel therefore influences all our thinking. For a baby, thinking involves being curious and making links.

## Making the inner world more realistic and protecting it

The inner world of babies and their lived experience intertwine in their developing minds.[1] Parents help their babies to differentiate a more realistic picture of the outside world and the contents of their mind. Babies want to relegate to the outside world what is unpleasant or does not fit with the existing inner picture, and they then realize that some of it needs to be taken back. This process continues as the inner world picture becomes more aligned with reality. The parents' response that feelings are meaningful and manageable focuses their baby's attention on internal experiences. One of the ways parents do this is by responding to babies' feelings with a similar but not exactly the same expression, so that babies realize that there is enough space to do this. If they are frightened and their parents replay a fear expression but vary it a little to show that they are not worried, their babies learn how to cope.

When parents help their babies differentiate what is inside their mind from what is outside, the world they live in becomes a less frightening one. It becomes easier to play and to symbolize as ways of dealing with difficulties and getting some distance from them. Parents try to help their babies feel that their internal world is safe and to protect their emerging thinking, imagination, and sense of self. This helps babies feel that it is safe to know their own mind and to have a consolidated sense of *going on being*—a sense of the self existing over time, with its own unique history. Babies can convey from age 5 months onwards, if not earlier, that they look for the mirroring-back and decoding of their emotional state on the faces of other people and have a sense of which people are more attuned than others to their inner state.

## Thinking

What has been called a jumble of fact and fantasy from the beginning gets gradually sorted out, and a baby develops representations or working models of the world. Experiences that babies have map onto innate preconceptions with which they have been born, like that of a virtual other into which the actual other steps.[2] That 2-month-old babies can readjust their gaze when an adult changes the direction of her gaze presupposes a world of objects existing in a space held in common.[3] Some thinking seems already to be starting *in utero.*

An early comparison that a baby may make is between his experience when he rushes to fill himself up at the breast and when he can drink more calmly and observe his mother seeing their relationship with her breast. The baby is then able to think about what is in her mind. This triadic way of functioning is a forerunner of the baby reaching out to involve a third person in the relationship he has with either parent.

A 6-month-old girl seemed to compare her observer with her mother. She started off recognizing the observer and being pleased to see her. She played up to her and continually looked back to her as if trying to work out her intentions and what she got from her. When she was in a swing and looked back, she did not smile much, as though she was still trying to work out what the observer was doing. She was more interested in looking at the observer than at her mother, and looked only fleetingly at her sister. She continued to check that the observer was watching her, but some of the joy of seeing her had worn off and she no longer seemed to want to show her anything. It was more as though she was wondering why the observer was still looking at her. Sometimes when she cried she appeared to be communicating that she was wondering whether the observer could understand what it was like for the baby. She seemed to think, "Those eyes see something different when they look at me from what my mother sees". As everyone was more active with her than the observer, her curiosity about the observer was stimulated and her representations about herself and other people seemed to become more differentiated.

On the other hand, when a child feels that the parents have been authoritarian, it may be harder to find a playful space with the parents and for thinking to become more elaborated.

## Sense of time

A baby gradually develops a sense of time that approaches what an adult's sense of time is like. To adults, a three-month delay in court proceedings is a manageable time frame—to a young child, it might be far too long to hold the image of the absent parent in mind. Tiny babies might only hold the picture of their absent mother for hours or days, an older baby for slightly longer. But as we will see in the next section, babies need the words to help this develop—such as "five more sleeps", with the fingers of the hand held up.

## Understanding language

As babies cannot usually say many words in the first year, it is easy to underestimate their understanding of language. From the beginning they are responsive to the tone in which words are spoken, as well as the intensity of feeling conveyed in them. At birth, babies have a universal tendency to discriminate the sounds of all languages, and they produce cooing sounds that are universal across cultures. By 2 months, babies can differentiate between recordings in which passages of speech are read either forwards or backwards, so they already know something about the structure of a normal language and know that backwards speech cannot be a normal language.[4]

By 12 weeks, they vocally imitate the vowel sounds of the language that they hear spoken, which will affect the kind of language they speak.[5] Well before babies learn to speak, they use words to help them make sense of the world. By 4 months, they are aware that people and things have labels, such as "dada". Babies of 9 months learn more about objects when these are labelled as belonging to a particular category. If babies are given word labels when they see or touch things, they pick out similarities with other objects more than do babies who do not hear objects named. They also sense the playfulness in the irony of an adult's comments, accompanied by rolling eyes and grimace, such as "that's a lovely hat Nanna is wearing, with the pretend birds on it".[6]

Girls develop speech faster than do boys, probably because as early as 6 months girls show left-hemisphere dominance—that is, more electrical activity in the left than in the right hemisphere when listening to speech sounds. A 6-month-old girl was able to accurately say "ted" for teddy and "jui" for juice.

Parents may feel that talking to babies about future events—a hospitalization, or a baby being born, or a pet that has to be put down—will not be understood, and yet something anticipatory gets communicated to them. The earlier a baby has opportunities to start connecting the words with what happens, the more helpful this seems. When babies are able to verbalize feelings they can use words as containers of strong feelings and fantasies. On the other hand, as they develop words, the part of them that used to be in a wordless communion with their parents feels as though it has been lost.[7]

As parents name feelings, babies can begin to think about being in an emotional relationship with another person. Some babies who were aged about 9 months with mild feeding refusal and who only said "da-da" and not "ma-ma" could start feeding when they were able to say the word "ma-ma".[8] Getting the word seemed to suggest that a link had been made in which they could take in from their mothers again. By 11 months, babies are aware when communication breaks down and possess strategies for repairing it. They may repeat the original attempt at communication, add gestures or emphasis, or substitute another word or gesture.[9]

A parent naming feelings helps a baby to develop the capacity of the mind to have insight into the feelings of the self and others. When a parent says "You're tired" (or bored, or cross, or angry, or sad), this is at the heart of the baby's developing reflective function. Children's attachment is linked with their capacity for self-reflective function. Their reflective function is an extremely important capacity in terms of secure attachment and sound mental health. Secure attachment is based on and leads to the capacity for reflection on the states of mind of the self and others.

Babies find it extremely hard when they sense that there are secrets that are not spoken about—as if something is so terrible that even their parents, as the giants protecting their world, are too frightened—and find this unbearable.

Children who cannot think about themselves and other people in an emotional relationship are not likely to be able to soothe themselves or talk about their distress.

## Conclusion

We have seen how much the feelings and fantasies that babies have intersect with their attempts to understand the world and how they have to disentangle them. At the same time, they face a succession of graded separations from their parents, who are usually their attachment figures. Even a holiday away from their home may be a kind of separation and could be bridged with photos of home.

# feeling good and feeling the best: healthy narcissism and omnipotence

Feeling good about the self is a developmental process that starts in the first year. This is a short chapter, but it describes an important aspect of a baby's first year.

## Feeling omnipotent and thinking magically

When babies sometimes think that they can make an event happen just by wishing it, they feel all-powerful. Not for nothing do parents talk about "His majesty, the king" when they attribute kingly powers to their baby. It is easy to see this with the toddler-aged child who crows, "I did it!" Babies who want a feed could imagine that, with the breast appearing when and where they want it, they make it happen, perhaps even that the breast is a part of them. (In the case of very young babies, they could feel this whether they are breastfed or bottle-fed.) When things go well, babies start off with a sense of "I created the world, I wanted the breast and I just made it happen, it just magically appeared right where I wanted it". There is both illusion and magical thinking.[1] The baby has created the illusion. It is the baby's magical thinking that made it happen. But when babies feel all-powerful, they then feel responsible for events that happen when they wished them to happen. While this is not easy to see in the first year, the roots are already there—feeling omnipotent and thinking magically are unlikely to appear out of nowhere in the second year.

Babies learn gradually in the first few months that they did not magically create their world, that some of it is not under their control but under their parents' control. Babies then have two streams of mental life available to them: the cognitive, intellectual one, and the creative one in which they can take refuge when they need a rest from reality.

## Consolidating self-esteem and narcissism

When things go well between parents and baby, a baby's self-esteem develops. Babies feel that they are understood and valued by the most important people in their world, who want them to feel good about themselves. They feel that they can entrance their parents, and this links with being able to be appropriately proud of themselves. From about 9 months onwards, babies' expressions and body language seem to say, "Look at me, world! Aren't I wonderful!" It is as though the world is their oyster. You can see this feeling expressed later in the nursery rhyme, "I'm the King of the Castle". For this part of development to go well, babies need to evoke appropriate responses from their parents so that they have a sense of efficacy as well as a sense of their self as a centre of initiative.

If babies have the sense that they created the breast just when and where they wanted it, they go through a period of disillusionment when they realize that they were not responsible for it. Around the age of 7 months, they start to realize that they are not the centre of the universe (although that does not stop them wanting to be the centre of their parents' attention).

Babies need to move on from thinking and wishing that they were at the centre of the universe. The normal omnipotence of this age needs to give way to a more reality-based view of the world and the baby's place in it. But when their experiences are those of "Want, want, want" and they feel that they "Get, get, get", this makes it hard for them to move forward developmentally. If parents feel that they have tended towards overgratifying their babies' wants and wishes rather than achieving an attuned and sensitive meeting of their baby's needs in the first six months, they can gently start to offer challenges that the baby can master with pride. Some babies find it hard to respond to the developmental challenge that frustration poses—not to respond with helplessness but with an active approach to solving the problem, to see facing reality as bringing its own excitement. However, when parents understand that this is what their baby is struggling with, they can help by presenting challenges in manageable doses and encouraging the baby with a sense of excitement about mastering these.

## Conclusion

When babies feel good about themselves, many benefits flow, such as a base for good self-esteem. Magical thinking and omnipotence are developmental stages that every baby passes through and are usually only reverted back to at a later stage under conditions of stress. Being able to cycle relatively easily from states of being invested in the self back to relatedness indicates a baby who is developing well. If babies can relinquish some of the magical thinking and self-centredness of this time, they will manage separation and other tasks of the first year better.

# 10

## concern and oedipal wishes

The early developments in intersubjective threesome communication contribute to a baby's developing concern for his parents. These developments also contribute to the baby's feelings and wishes about being at times included in a couple's closeness and at times excluded from it. Some babies seem easily able to let another person come into their relationship with one other person, some babies find it very hard to share.[1] Over their first year, babies discriminate more about whom they reach out to and how they do so. Early in the year they reach out to include whoever seems to be left out. But within a few months they seem to reach out specifically to certain people in a way that is often different from how they are with most other people in their environment. Several male observers have reported girl babies aged about 15 weeks acting in a flirtatious way with them;[2] female observers have also commented on both girl and boy babies behaving in a more excited way with them than with their fathers or siblings.

## Developing concern

Throughout the first year, babies' caring feelings for their parents become consolidated. These include their love and enjoyment of their parents and gratitude for what their parents give them. Their feelings also include wanting not to hurt their parents and sadness at being hurtful, even if it was only in thought. Angry thoughts and feelings about their parents may become quite passionate. As their parents are also the people whom babies love the most in the world, making the connection about being angry with their parents leads to the babies being upset. They then seem at times to be low-keyed or even sad. This contributes to their feeling of being concerned about their parents, and it forms the basis for the urge to make reparation when babies feel that another person has been hurt or injured. Babies generalize this feeling of not wanting to hurt their parents to not wanting to hurt other people with whom they are less closely connected. It becomes a precursor for the feeling of guilt. Partly because it may link with depressive feelings later in life, it has been called the *depressive position*.[3] Another way of looking at it is the struggle between selfishness and unselfishness.

## Oedipal feelings

Love for other people leads a baby into potential competition and rivalries. The Greek myth of Oedipus is used to refer to those wishes that the child has for the parent of the opposite sex when the child has turned away from the parent of the same sex. Oedipus was an adopted child who, as an adult, inadvertently married his biological mother after having inadvertently killed his biological father. Oedipal wishes here refer to girls as well as boys, while acknowledging that girls cannot have exactly the same experiences as boys in terms of the new identifications they make and the early ones they modify. Oedipal feelings are not the regressed feelings of the ill child who wants comfort from the mother, nor those of the child who turns away temporarily from a parent who has been a cause of disappointment. Rather, coping with oedipal wishes is a developmental step to be negotiated by all babies.

These wishes can easily be seen around the age of 3 years. One little girl said, "I love you, Mummy. It's just that I love Daddy more." Another boy told his father that when he was grown up he would marry Mummy. His father replied that when he was grown up he would have a girlfriend of his own. The boy responded, "You marry her, Daddy, and I'll marry Mummy."

But these wishes seem to be present even earlier than 3 years. Babies of around 6 to 8 months of age at times turn from the same-sex parent and make it clear that they prefer the parent of the opposite sex. Babies from this age onwards struggle with feelings of sometimes being the one who is left out and sometimes the one doing the leaving out, which may feel hurtful. (These feelings can be seen in the early signs of jealousy in twins.)

Some of the changes in these feelings about being in a twosome and threesome were seen in a little girl with her male observer. When she was 14 weeks old, she began giving him huge smiles and was more interested in him than her mother. Two weeks later, she was so loving and playful that he felt like laughing and picking her up. Her interest in him continued for the next three months, and she would strain to turn around and look at him. Her mother thought that this relationship paralleled the one her daughter had with her father but that it had its own unique quality as well.

Often after the baby had given up trying to get him to play an escalating game of smiling, she engaged him with intense eye contact. He would look away after about twenty seconds, and she began to imitate this behaviour, with a dream-like reflective look. She muted her response, as though she felt that there was something wrong with it. She seemed to wonder what he was thinking. Her mother noticed that she went into this space by herself. It had a more active thinking quality than daydreaming. When she was 5 months old and he talked to her mother, she felt ignored and burst into hurt tears. Two months later, she seemed to feel certain situations, such as being put to bed, as a rejection. She made a considerable effort to contain these feelings and began, with precocious independence, to sing herself to sleep. At 8 months of age, she rapidly weaned herself, as if rejecting her mother, and also turned away from the observer with an embarrassed, coy smile.

Gradually babies realize that sometimes they are not in the forefront of their parents' mind and actions. Babies vary enormously in how they respond to being excluded. It is a major developmental task that they face, and how they resolve it is important for subsequent mental health. Some babies are able to take it in their stride and wait patiently until their parents, or the couple excluding them, are ready to turn their attention back to them. For other babies, it hurts their self-esteem very much and pushes them to face the narcissistic hurt of not being omnipotent. This waiting and watching, provided babies can do it in a relatively calm and thoughtful way, is an important part of being able to observe and reflect on what happens emotionally between people. The oedipal situation is a developmental step when, if children can tolerate the separateness of the parental couple and the loss of exclusive possession of their mother that it implies, they gain a perspective that takes account of other people's viewpoints, which is essential in their future relationships. They gain the capacity to be separate from significant people in their life and to reflect on themselves.

These developments begin in the first six months, although there cannot be a precise time-line as there would be with motor and cognitive milestones. The achievements of a secure attachment are similar to the achievements of the stage of concern. Having achieved this higher level, along with appropriate opportunities for gratitude and grief, a baby can begin to tolerate compromise. One of the more mature emotions is forgiveness. Some babies are temperamentally very easygoing and generous, which makes it particularly easy for the parents to respond to them as if they were forgiving, and for the babies to develop forgiveness. The mother of an 11-week-old girl said that she looked so frightened and vulnerable and screamed inconsolably when an ointment stung her that she hoped her baby would not think that she hurt her on purpose, and she was relieved when the baby subsequently smiled at her radiantly. A child who can forgive is on the way to overcoming humiliation, resentment, and anger.

## Difficulties in the oedipal stage

A less mature state for the child is holding onto a grievance or continuing with a sense of entitlement, which can easily slide into states of feeling threatened and blamed. These latter states would be an *all-or-nothing* state or an *either–or* state: "I should get everything that I want or I'm not having anything to do with it." Humans have evolved to have *both–and* minds, rather than either–or ones. The latter state of mind is familiar to parents who have been confronted by a child's imperiousness that brooks no denial or a child's completely black-and-white view of a situation. Another way of putting it from the young child's perspective is contrasting a *now-or-never* state of mind about time with one that can envisage *now-as-well-as-later*.

Towards the end of the first year, a child who feels that another child might take his mother away can very clearly signal distress and displeasure about this. If a baby's mother plays with a large doll, the baby may have the same response of jealousy, shown in crying or protesting in anger, hitting or biting her or clinging to her or engaging in self-comforting behaviour.[4] The baby is saying, "She's mine", which is another version of oedipal feelings.

If young children feel they have sided with one parent against another parent, this can be frightening for them. Babies can usually discriminate run-of-the-mill arguments between the parents that get resolved, but they may be very affected by and worried about ongoing rowing of the more serious kind. If they are on the look out for what is happening between the parents and preoccupied about it, it is hard for them to get on with their own spontaneous playing.

## Beginnings of a value system or conscience

It may be hard to observe the beginnings of a conscience or value system in the first year. An 11-month-old girl crawled towards a wastepaper bin and, before exploring it, turned to her mother to read her expression, checking the external rules. Values and internal rules have, however, to start somewhere, and they have their roots in this year.

One of the most important achievements for parents is to help their children take ownership of their conscience. One of the first phrases parents teach their babies is to say "thank you", or a variation on this. Being grateful is one of the single most important elements in human relationships—recognizing when another person has been kind or is owed a debt of gratitude.

Parents work hard to teach their babies to be aware when they do something that hurts another person. Often these acts are unintentionally hurtful, perhaps when a baby reaches out to catch hold of another person. The sentence, "That hurts him", which attempts to build on empathy for other people, is very important for a sense of morality. When babies feel concerned about having had hurtful thoughts about their parents, this is the first step towards building up an internal voice that guides them in living ethically.

What babies need in the beginning from their parents is an attuned meeting of their needs, gradually shading into an appropriate meeting of them—in other words, not gratifying them on every occasion. Sometimes this means letting babies cry for a few minutes to see if they will settle. It means parents feeling comfortable to be firm and saying "no" at times. Rules that keep babies safe have to be non-negotiable. All of this acts as a base for babies to take over a set of values to structure their lives. Both parents contribute to this, with mothers often providing this structure on a more continuous day-to-day basis.

Parents work towards helping their children gradually take responsibility for their own conscience and system of values. Sometimes parents and children may face difficulties in jointly negotiating this. When parents are able to avoid getting into unnecessary battles, it is easier for children to develop their own set of internal rules. If children feel that they are told off frequently or that their parents are authoritarian, some fight back and so avoid having to accept their own feelings of guilt and what they need to do to live at peace with their own conscience. A pattern may get set up of them fighting with their parents, who are seen as horrible and witch-like and whom they later feel justified in defying.

Alternatively, if babies feel that their parents intervene too much, they may defer to their parents and later may be bossy with their peers in the same way that they felt their parents were with them. This is similar to what may happen if toilet training is started too strictly and too early, even though initially it may appear to bring good results. Too-structured a training may put in place a kind of bedrock in their inner life that privileges rules rather than the freedom of thought that they will need later on. What is important is the way in which they take over being responsible for this and for other rules imposed on them.

## Conclusion

Children's capacity to be concerned for the feelings of others, and to take responsibility if they feel that they have hurt someone, are moral achievements. Coping with feelings about sometimes being excluded from a couple's activities contributes to the process of a child being able to have a thoughtful perspective on life.

part **III**

# THE SELF IN DIFFICULTY

". . . no language but a cry"
Alfred, Lord Tennyson[1]

The bonding that parents seek at birth may take longer with premature babies or with those who need special care. Attachment behaviour increases when a baby is tired, sick, or in pain. The anxiety that babies experience is about trying to keep their parents and themselves connected. If their parents can comfort them, their distress and anxiety recedes. The problems described in this chapter usually mean that some of the feeding and sleeping difficulties mentioned earlier have been exacerbated.

# physical and emotional difficulties

## Pain, illness, or disability

The majority of babies experience minor illnesses and procedures in the first year. Most babies who have heel pricks and
injections in their first year tolerate this well, and some use
these experiences of invasive procedures to make a developmental move forward. Other babies seem so sensitive that
having an invasive procedure feels as though it should not have
happened, that it is too much to cope with, and they regress
temporarily. If parents are able to think about the effect an
intervention is having, despite any distress they themselves may
feel, their babies usually can too, without it being traumatic.

A simple cold may have a considerable effect on babies in
the first few months, resulting in regression and in expressing
their feelings less vigorously. Such regression as a response to
illness allows a baby a rest from the demands of life, even if
occasionally it may look as though the baby does not regain the
ground lost for quite some time.

We can only begin to imagine what the experience of being
seriously unwell or suffering a disability feels like. Even a newborn baby can respond to a threat to survival with enormous
anxiety. Some parents feel that when invasive procedures are
done to their baby, they would like to be there for support.

Others cannot bear to see their babies hurt, or they fear that their babies may associate them with the hurting. There is no single right or correct way. If parents could feel that what matters is to find what works best for them and their baby—and realize that they usually know their baby better than anyone—this would guide them in providing the support their baby needs. Their baby's personality and past history, as well as those of their parents', would then point to what the babies would find most supportive. For some babies, if at all possible the parents need to be present so that the baby can keep his gaze locked on them. Other babies manage better if they have their transitional object during the procedure and their parents are there to greet them in a less frazzled state after it is completed.

Nothing prepares a parent to have a baby who is born ill or physically or intellectually disabled. When babies are nursed in neonatal intensive care units, the nurses suggest that even if touch is too painful for them, babies are very responsive to the gaze of their parents and therefore feel sustained by it. The nurses feel that the babies express their feelings by sneezing, vomiting, giving a violent kick, or withdrawing. These babies have so many heel pricks that they quickly learn to resist when their heel is grasped.

Babies need their parents (and nurses) to hold the balance between despair and hope, not to join with the despair—in which case they would feel lost in it—but able to keep alive some hope to which they would be sensitive in the adult's voice and touch.

Attachment issues are important for such babies, who are often handled by up to forty staff members a day. The stress of hospital conditions sometimes interferes with parents' attachment to their babies, whom they may feel belong to the hospital. But many parents become extraordinarily devoted: they allow their babies to regress, to be by themselves, to tune-out for brief periods of time.[1] Very compromised babies, in order to survive, cannot experience fully all that goes on around them; some withdrawal is essential. This helps explain how some babies who have suffered trauma can become integrated children.

## When there are emotional difficulties

Babies may have difficulties in their relationships with their parents for a number of reasons. These include constitutional factors such as an inhibited or difficult temperament, as well as factors of an environmental nature, and how all these mesh together. There may be difficulties in the fit between babies and other important people in their world. There may be traumatic events compounding the picture. When parents think about what their babies need, it is helpful to consider whether in other areas they are doing well or seem generally to be stuck.

## Adopted and fostered babies

While many adoptions offer the best outcome for a baby, an adopted baby may have a particular vulnerability. Even at age 10 days, babies will register a difference in change of caregivers, although girls' biological rhythms are not as disrupted as boys' are.[2] This suggests that while later there will not be a conscious memory of losing the biological parent(s), there may be a bodily trace that stays as a vulnerability, so that the babies are slightly less resilient, as a result of having lost the mother who carried them. This may have been underestimated.

Sometimes a baby has experienced traumatic events before the adoption, and the adoptive parents are then met with fear and rejection. But the biological imperative for babies is to turn to those who provide love and care, so that, whatever the early difficulties, they turn to the adoptive parents, needing them to be their psychological parents, to be parents who are emotionally meaningful for them.

## Being born after a bereavement

A baby who is born after miscarriages or deaths may collect a lot of feelings about being the baby who takes the place of the dead baby or other person. Parents may find it hard for some time to see their baby in his own right and not as the child whose place he is felt to take. The baby may feel that, as he is not that person, he is not welcomed or valued, which may contribute to his being anxious. While this often does not show until later, some babies are very sensitive to this in the first year, and, if their parents suffer with unresolved grief and anger, babies may take it as directed against them. If they misread the anger as directed towards them, they may respond by becoming inhibited and lacking joy in life.

## Response to traumatic events

For babies, a traumatic event temporarily overwhelms their ways of coping. Many of the experiences described in this chapter may feel traumatic to babies. Some babies find a short separation traumatic if they are left with a stranger while their parents are away, whereas other babies can take it more in their stride.

Babies' responses indicate when they have found experiences traumatic. In the first six months, a baby may be hyperalert, dysregulated, irritable, withdrawn, or easily startled. In the second six months, a baby may, in addition, be very much more anxious in strange situations, have more specific angry reactions in particular situations, show more active attempts to avoid specific situations, and display developmental regressions and sleep disorders. These responses, if severe enough, may indicate that babies are suffering from what would in an older child be regarded as post-traumatic stress disorder.

## "Ghosts in the nursery"

The evocative phrase "ghosts in the nursery"[3] describes the ghosts of difficulties from the parents' past, the traumas that have been unresolved, that may rise up again and frighten parents away from their children. When something in a baby intersects with experiences for their parents that are painful or anxiety provoking, it affects how they are with their baby and also makes it central for the baby, magnifying the experience.

New parents feel that there are many anxieties waiting to trip them up. As with Sleeping Beauty, a bad fairy-godmother waiting in the wings is always a possibility, in the anxieties that mothers have that something bad will happen to their babies, or they will be angry with their babies, or their babies will die. Mothers often feel guilty, fearing that they have failed their babies and not been perfect.

## Being with a mother who is depressed

Many mothers who suffer depression in the first year of their baby's life, or are ill in other ways, have times when they are less responsive to their babies. For some mothers, however, the depressive feelings do not centre on their baby but on another aspect of their life.

For babies, if their mother's face is not responsive or available, the process of them finding themselves in the expression on their mother's face may be interrupted, and this influences how they see themselves and contributes to a loss of hope.

Babies have many ways of responding to the experience of their mother's depression. Some babies by the age of 6 weeks seem to feel that the joy has been taken out of their life, and they may identify with her depressed mood or try to cheer her up.

To balance what has been said, some babies whose mothers suffer from depressed feelings may also be more alert, sensitive, creative, and attuned to other people's emotional states. Babies who have had periods of being anxious may also develop these sensitivities. The experience of being in touch so closely with the suffering of someone important to them may stem from a special sensitivity and also foster this sensitivity.

Babies may be affected by their mother's depression and anxiety before they are born, and at birth they may be less active and less alert.[4] If babies become depressed, they may have difficulty eating or sleeping and become miserable or shut down. They can look sullen and push people away, and it is hard to be sympathetic to a baby who acts like this. This is different from those times when a baby's anxiety is covered up protectively by being angry. Babies may reject, in the sense of pushing the other person away first so as to avoid the rejection that they are frightened is about to happen. Whereas girls are more self-contained, boys tend to be more dependent on their mothers for help in managing their feelings of joy and anger; when they have depressed mothers, boys seem to feel more angry and deprived.

When babies feel that they are not in their parents' mind and could therefore get lost, they feel extremely threatened. If unrelieved, this state can be traumatic. Parents may feel very preoccupied with a number of severe stressors, such as being ill or burdened in other ways. When a baby continues to feel stressed, production of cortisol, a stress hormone, is increased; over time this has an effect on the brain's structure and metabolism and may make for later difficulties, such as, for example, a type of attention deficit hyperactivity disorder. As help for these and related difficulties is available so that they do not become fixed, parents can keep a watching brief if they think that there are difficulties in the baby's life which could affect him or if they are alerted by behavioural signs. These might include a baby being very anxious and jittery, or being very wary and alert, or, conversely, tuning-out a lot and so losing the chance to process incoming information. And when babies' motor activity comes more under their control, they may rush headlong into things in a way that feels breathless to the onlooker, as though there is very little space for calmly assessing the situation.

## Responding to trauma in the relationship

For some parents who had difficult and frightening childhoods, such experiences may still be very alive, and their baby may remind them of some aspects. When parents respond to their baby in a frightened or frightening way that has more to do with their past than the with baby in front of them, the baby senses it and becomes terrified in turn. Where parents look at their baby, they may see instead someone from their past who frightened them. But a 6-week-old baby registers only the look on a caregiver's face of fear or anger, a look that lasts a quarter of a second (which adults would be unable to see unaided). This helps to explain how the effects of parents' traumatic childhoods can be transmitted down through the generations.

Babies who see one of their parents being threatened find it traumatic that a parent who is supposed to protect them has not been able to protect him/herself. Because babies are tiny and vulnerable, they are initially passive onlookers. Some then respond in a more active way by identifying with the person whom they perceive to be aggressive. Some babies seem to feel that the best way that they can manage to cope is to act like the big person who is a threat. Babies then potentially have both responses—being aggressive and being a victim—available for their later development, although if they feel that things go well for them, neither response may be activated.

Those babies who withdraw when they feel terrified and are in a constant state of being persecuted are mostly those who *have* suffered considerably from neglect or abuse. They then try to cope by becoming hyper-alert or by cutting-off. Babies who feel that they are not liked usually end up being hateful and then feel they have wiped everything out and feel empty.

## Coping in ways that constrict

"Coping" is used in the sense of using personal resources to manage experiences that generate tension. One way of coping is by being very good. Some babies are already noticeably so good by 3 weeks of age that the nurses looking after their mothers, who had a breakdown after the babies' birth, comment that the babies seem to know they need to be good.[5] Other babies may be compliant without it having a marked effect on their development. But sometimes babies cover their true self protectively behind a protective shell until it feels safe enough to emerge.

All tiny babies interrupt their gazing at their parents and turn away so as not to feel overwhelmed, and doing this is a sign of health. But some babies use gaze-avoidance too often and lose opportunities to engage in a joyful way with the world. Parents usually have a sense that their baby is refusing eye contact more than they intuitively feel is appropriate, and that trying to engage with their baby's gaze has become a manoeuvre to "chase and grab" the baby's attention rather than a pleasurable experience for them both. Babies may differ in the way they gaze-avert. Some may always look away to the left or to the right, some may have a dulling in their eyes, some look at their parents when they are looking away, and some may be selective about whom they look at and whom they do not. The longer babies avoid the gaze of their parents and other people, the greater the possibility that it will begin to affect how they learn. What starts off descriptively looking like an autistic way-of-being with other people may, without help, become fixed in several years' time as a way of cutting-off.

Some babies seem to have no fear, which may in part be a temperamental trait. It may, however, indicate that babies are denying fear and rushing into situations in which they would be most frightened. Babies resort to precocious independence to reassure themselves that they can manage by themselves.

The more worrying ways that a baby has of coping in the first year fall broadly within the *hypervigilant* or *dissociation* categories. Stilling and freezing are defences that indicate a baby's extreme anxiety. The challenge for the parents is in deciding whether their baby's development is progressing satisfactorily in an overall way or whether it should be assessed to see if an intervention would help. Behaviours that may look worrying at the beginning of the year may look very different later on. One example of this was when the mother of a 3-month-old daughter said, "She's asleep while she's awake." With dissociation, babies tune out, usually with their eyes glazed or turned away; it is as matter of concern if babies resort to this a lot. This little girl, however, only needed to use it for a certain period early in her development, and a few months later she looked happy and well-related.

In another case, a 6-week-old girl often slept motionless with her hands in the air, like a frozen coiled spring, a hypervigilant response that did not let her relax even in sleep. While some babies sleep in this way, this baby's mother was single and unsupported and had other significant stresses. Over the next few months, however, the baby made a good adaptation to her life circumstances, showing considerable resilience.

Lastly, an 8-month-old girl sat motionless for twenty minutes on a couch while her parents were interviewed, whereas a baby of this age would not usually sit still for so long. Not only was the normal activity of this age seriously curtailed, but she also needed to be on her guard in a hypervigilant way. In this case, she and her parents were assessed as needing a therapeutic intervention, from which they benefited.[6]

If babies need to use these defences extensively it is more hopeful if they can find a flexible balance between using hypervigilance and dissociation rather than using only one or the other. When these defences become more marked or are the only response at difficult times, babies are communicating that they need help. The most extreme response is a kind of disintegration, in which babies let go of internal psychological structures but usually regroup later.

Much of what has been described can make parents and babies very sad, and it is important to know that there is a range of ways to help them, one of the most important being to provide support for mothers who are sad and depressed. If parents can come to see how early their baby interacts socially with them and with other people, this can also be enormously helpful for them. I believe that this is the single most important message that parents could take from this book.

## Infant–parent psychotherapy

Infant–parent psychotherapy takes place either in sessions with parents and babies present or in a therapy group. When adults relate to babies with play that is thoughtfully about them, the babies have a sense of being "met" and this conveys hope to them and their parents.

Offering sessions for parents and their baby is a more common approach than group work. With infant–parent psychotherapy, parents may be offered a range of different approaches, ranging from more explorative to more focused methods. With a more explorative approach, parents and babies might be offered between four and ten sessions to understand how past difficulties are influencing the present ones. With more focused approaches, the number of sessions offered is usually shorter and may include the use of video-taping to provide helpful feedback.

Clinicians try to include the babies—however young they are—as much as the parents in the session, and they are related to as subjects in their own right. Clinicians put into words for the parents what they think the babies are feeling and thinking and try also to convey this to the babies and to relate to them on that basis. The clinicians try to help the parents understand why they are feeling the way they are feeling in the light of their own personal history. When the clinicians convey to the babies that they are thinking about them as a subject in their own right, and with a mind to register the emotional consequences of any impingement and any interaction, the results can be quite dramatic.

Weekly therapy groups for parents and infants may be more supportive for some babies and their parents. These follow the core principle of infant–parent psychotherapy—that is, that the infant is equally a focus of the intervention as the parents are. In the protected, confidential space of a group, as well as the interventions from the clinicians there is support from the other parents. One mother in a group said, "Twelve months ago I didn't have any love for my daughter, it was like a duty. This was the only place I felt I got help. A lot of the time I felt terrible, I wanted to die, I wished she was dead, and I didn't feel courageous enough to say it. Sometimes everything seems so bad like you're drowning in the midst of chaos." As her daughter's symptoms resolved, the little girl reached out in a very therapeutic way to the other infants in the group, which is a general feature of the infant–infant interaction in a group.

Sometimes very ill and depressed babies are referred for help, and even a brief contact with a clinician in which an alive, meaningful contact is made may be enough to reverse the cycle of despair and start the baby's development moving forwards again.

With one baby, who the medical staff thought was dying even though his liver transplant was successful, the clinician suggested to his mother that he was depressed, and she said, "I hadn't thought of that ever, but now you mention it, of course."[7] In this way she was beginning to think of her baby in a different way. And then the baby, enlivened by the contact with the clinician, started to reach out to his mother. It was as though no one had quite believed that there was a meaning behind the way he presented, but now they could see this there was hope. He then started to play, his face transformed by brilliant smiles, and he subsequently recovered quickly, both physically and psychologically.

One mother said, after this kind of help, "The things that were causing the grief and distress—I've met them and worked through them . . . and feel I've come out the other side. . . . Now I play with her . . . she's lovely, and I didn't have those feelings last year . . . our relationship is different, and I feel I love her."

The whole first year is an extraordinary one in terms of the consolidation of development on the journey that babies have accomplished from birth. Babies need their parents to see them both for the independent explorers that they are, wanting to make their own relationships and make their own way in the world, as well as for the tiny babies that they are, still very much in need of cradling and scaffolding.

# the search for ariadne's thread—
# the first year of life

CLAUS G. H. NEWMAN

The euphoria following the birth of a baby is remarkable and tends to obscure most of the negative feelings of doubt and uncertainty that may have intruded, unbidden, during the months of expectancy. In some developed societies, however, the prevalent pattern of care suggests that professionals may have hijacked the family support for the new parents to develop confidence in their capacity to care for the baby. Two predictable results followed from the medicalization of pregnancy and childbirth. The first is the welcome drop in infant morbidity and mortality, to which improved living conditions and parental nutrition have also contributed. The second is unwelcome—namely, a view that decisions in day-to-day problems of infant care can only be achieved with the provision of professional opinion. This picture is varied, with a return to more non-professional arrangements in some places. Perhaps this is a consequence of ever-shorter hospital stays following delivery and also, probably, an expression of the increasing popularity of "natural" patterns of childbirth.

Dr Claus G. H. Newman is an eminent paediatrician who worked as a Consultant to Westminster Medical School and Queen Mary's Hospital, Roehampton. It was in the latter that he ran the service for thalidomide children that acquired national and international prominence. He also works as an expert consultant to the Courts.

123

Rest following labour and delivery, with relief from other responsibilities while in hospital, used to extend for four to six days. This allowed the mother full concentration on the new situation as well as her recuperation, with the added benefit of ready help being available (at least in well-staffed units) for the beginning of infant feeding by breast or bottle, or both. Staff shortages and cuts in health service provision resulted in return to home after only a few hours following delivery, and this devolves the responsibility of care back to the family and community services. Unfortunately, present living patterns involve a dispersal of the wider family, as well as increasing numbers of single-parent families. This has made the return home a potentially stressful and lonely experience, with the added responsibility for the care of the new infant, quite often with no family model for the mother to remember. Visits by the community midwife and later by the health visitor, and information regarding clinics and parent groups provided by these professionals or the GP, all provide some support. But in many years of practice as a paediatrician, when clinics were made available according to local need and without waiting lists, I found that there was no lack of anxious parents requiring advice and reassurance concerning almost all normal aspects of a baby's life. However, very often the expressed fear of illness was not a result of symptoms of some abnormal condition but, rather, arose from what appeared to me a sense of insecurity stemming from an underlying experience of isolation and helplessness.

Irrespective of the development of present and future patterns of health care for parents with new babies, it seems to me that existing "baby books" include advice on "what to do if . . .", and how to manage different situations, but rather less on how to regain adult confidence in this supremely important role.

"Is my baby normal?" remains a major preoccupation, perhaps because the medical model of giving advice is a response to parents voicing their anxiety that something may be wrong.

Parents always wish to talk to someone with appropriate experience about their new baby. Sadly, duty schedules and involvement in problems affecting other patients may well militate against such a wish being met, as it should be, by obstetricians, midwives, or paediatricians. In fact, anecdotal evidence suggests that ancillary hospital staff, such as cleaners, as well as other mothers tend to provide important if unpaid support here.

The baby's normality is evaluated by an assessment immediately after birth; there is then a later one once the baby's physiology can be studied. In the former, the reaction to the delivery and the external appearance give much information, but some particular elements must be looked for. With the present pattern of only a few hours in hospital, an initial assessment of the baby—with knowledge of relevant medical facts from the pregnancy, the mother's health, and the family history— is all that is possible. The later assessment in the community will include an evaluation of the baby's weight and size, his alertness, muscle tone and activity, sleeping and waking pattern, interest in and capacity to feed, indications of a normal circulation and lung function, to name but a few elements. Parents will generally not analyse such distinct aspects but will respond to their baby instinctively as bonding becomes established. This process of mutual adaptation develops gradually and has no "normal" time limit. Each mother–baby pair follows their own needs and abilities. Sometimes, when the mother has previously enjoyed a non-domesticated and independent lifestyle, a greater adjustment to the new role comes to be required and this may extend the period of bonding.

Feeding patterns may at times be difficult to establish, and it is here that the ultra-short hospital stay has an important disadvantage. Breast engorgement, with discomfort or pain and little or no secretion on the second day after delivery, is followed by milk engorgement, after which proper lactation can progress, with the baby being the best possible means for emptying the breast. Some babies are quiet, others tend to cry often, and some mothers find themselves interpreting the baby's behaviour as a measure of their competence as mothers. Negotiating these first few days can be very stressful and can cause sleeplessness and feelings of depression. This is when experienced support can be of immense help. Some mothers have a firm idea of how their babies should be fed, while others are influenced by family or friends' beliefs on the importance of breastfeeding, and, if breastfeeding is not successful, they can feel they have failed. From a medical point of view, if both mother and baby are happy, and the baby is gaining weight adequately on breast milk or an appropriate alternative, then further paediatric input is unnecessary. Nevertheless, clinic facilities should be available for advice as necessary, immunization, and a check on normal developmental progress.

As regards the baby's weight, after an initial loss of less than 10% of birth-weight, feeding and therefore weight gain should become established within the first week in a full-term baby. An easily remembered approximation of expected gain is about 30 grams (about 1 ounce) a day or 180–210 grams (about 6–7 ounces) per week for the first three months, then about half a kilogram (about 1 pound) per month up to the first birthday. Such approximations reflect the slowing-down of the infant's initial rapid rate of growth. The importance of a normal weight gain can hardly be overemphasized. When within normal parameters of weight gain, most serious illnesses can be safely excluded, but when there is failure to gain weight adequately, in most instances an informed review of feeding will be all that is necessary to restore healthy growth.

In my experience, there is a widespread and inappropriate expectation that growth and weight charts must remain in the province of professionals. Simply used, such records can prevent undue prolongation of involuntary underfeeding, can provide useful reassurance of normal progress, and, rarely, can provide early warning of the need for professional advice. Having weighing scales at home can be very helpful, but for some parents they can become the source of much unnecessary anxiety. It may be useful to discuss this with the family doctor or the paediatrician.

Effective infant feeding requires a sufficient supply of milk. How much is enough? If the feeds are not unduly prolonged, and allow a period of rest both for the baby and for the mother before the next feed, and the baby is gaining weight satisfactorily, then it is very likely that the baby is getting enough milk. If, however, feeds take too long, or if weight gain is unsatisfactory, then an insufficiency of the amount of milk either being offered or getting into the baby is likely. The technique of breast- or bottle-feeding is a large subject. The help of a patient and experienced family member, friend, or professional can be of vital importance here. Green, mucousy (i.e. unmixed with yellow food residue) stools before the introduction of mixed feeding will mostly occur with underfeeding from any cause and are not a sign of infection. Air swallowing is common and can be a major cause of paroxysms of crying related to feeds as the air passes through the bowel. The baby will pass this air when having a bowel motion, so it is easy to detect. Babies learn quickly, and the expectation of pain to follow a feed may make further feeding more difficult. Avoidance of air swallowing would be the logical response, but this can be difficult to achieve. With bottle-fed babies, one of the most rewarding bits of advice I have ever given is to make sure that the teat holes are large enough to allow a continuous stream of milk when the bottle is up-ended. If the milk falls drop-wise, the holes are most probably too small. When breastfeeding, it is the fit between the baby's lips and the mother's nipple and areola that determines the effectiveness of the feeding. It is, therefore, important to seek this matching by trying different postures and positions until a satisfactory feeding position is found.

Another unnecessary worry is whether it is "alright" to mix breast- with bottle-feeding. It is perfectly "alright", provided that it suits both mother and baby! There may be consequences, in that one or the other method may come to be preferred. When mothers are away working during the day, a breastfeed first thing in the morning and last thing at night, with artificial feeds during the day at nursery, works well. It did so for innumerable mothers whose babies were looked after in nurseries during the 1939–45 war years.

Further worries concern the possible content of poisonous substances (e.g. aluminium), or the lack of the most appropriate vitamins and other factors, in infant feeds. It is important to remember that the current generation of adults is living increasingly long lives, despite exposure to poisons or lacks that were unknown to our parents when we were infants. The news of some new threat presently appears to last only a few weeks before it disappears into the professional literature. While most parents will rightly wish to be informed should a real advance occur, I suspect that a fairly laid-back attitude is the right one

Fashionable supposed causes of disorders can also cause unnecessary worry. There are, indeed, some babies who react adversely, for example, to the protein in cow's milk. If such fears are held or there are feeding problems of one sort or another, professional help should be sought to prove or disprove them. With this in mind, it is better to keep baby feeds very simple, with few or no additives other than the traditional vitamins, for the first six months.

Perhaps the least acknowledged but deepest concern relates to development. Since the future of a new baby can seldom be predicted, any major negative factor such as disease, serious handicap, and the likelihood of serious learning difficulty are commonly regarded with suppressed or rarely expressed fear, even when there are already other affected family members. The problem is deepened by the widely varying patterns of normal development and the length of observation and experience necessary before professionals can give meaningful opinions. A frequent difficulty is that of denial, whereby comforting explanations are offered by the closest relatives, trying to counterbalance the views of more distant relatives or friends that something is wrong. Less experienced professionals may also compound such difficulties, since specialized expertise is required to clarify these cases. However, despite all these considerations, there are signs that most parents pick up naturally from their new babies and from which they develop appropriate confidence. I suspect that at times this important process is not helped by indiscriminate non-professional reading, since only the correct interpretation of the relevant features of the baby will allay the parents' anxieties.

The signs of positive health and of normal development are easier to experience than to describe. Some of the main developmental milestones are:

- the establishment of feeding and weight gain
- evidence of awareness on the baby's part of the mother's nearness
- quieting in mother's arms
- a wish for closeness
- eyes moving in the direction of new sounds and, later, the distinction between meaningful and unmeaning background sound
- moving all four limbs and development of purposive movement, but without any clear preference for left or right before age 2 years
- developing a regular sleeping–waking pattern
- crying not continuous but at least potentially related to hunger, bowel or bladder activity, or other sensory stimuli (too cold? too hot?).

Finally, at this very early stage, the "social smile" at about six weeks after term delivery, with its profound effect on bonding, evidences a great deal of normality. In my opinion, all the above are best experienced without any need for professional explanation, though the background State organizations can strongly reassure and encourage vulnerable parents by confirmation of good and normal progress. The habit of baby clinic attendance is a good one, provided that there is not too much staff turnover and the possibility is encouraged of forging links between parents and a health visitor or doctor. Concern about possible problems continues throughout childhood and beyond—but perhaps this is an intrinsic part of parenthood?

The role of advice giving and of "authority" figures has changed markedly over the last thirty to forty years. The problem has many facets, but the effects are that parents are making choices they are not trained to make, as a result of mistrust of just those people who should have the appropriate information on which to base advice. The controversy regarding immunization against measles, mumps, and German measles is a recent example, where I believe many parents have disadvantaged their children because of the premature publication of misleading medical opinions.

Public health problems such as the BSE cattle epidemic, with human victims of new variant Creutzfeld–Jakob disease, have magnified the problem of lack of confidence in authority. Unfortunately, areas of knowledge such as immunity are unbelievably complex, so that as regards immunization, the doctors and nurses advising parents, while having considerable knowledge of the subject, still need to take much on trust from established and, in their view, trustworthy sources. These sources may at times disagree, and established views may change over the decades, though many views remain unchanged. Publicity requires simplification, and I believe that it is impossible to present highly complex issues in simple sound-bites, rather than in well-planned programmes. Should the media therefore report that someone is claiming a link between something that affects many people and some unhappy outcome, it is hard to see how such an evil genie can be put back into the bottle, other than waiting for the incident to be forgotten in the shadow of the next "exposé". I forget which came first—was it that autism was being caused by immunization, or that aluminium in infant feeds was poisoning our babies? The identification of the research papers concerned, followed by a definitive view by a small number of "ultra-experts" with the ability to handle and comment on the information, linked to consequent public safety legislation, might be a way forward.

## Chapter 1

1. D. W. Winnicott. "Primary maternal pre-occupation" (1956). In: *Collected Papers: Through Paediatrics to Psychoanalysis* (London: Tavistock Publications, 1958).

2. B. D. Perry, R. A. Pollard, T. L. Blakley, W. L. Baker, & D. Vigilante. "Childhood trauma, the neurobiology of adaptation, and 'use-dependent' development of the brain: How 'states' become 'traits'." *Infant Mental Health Journal, 16* (1995): 271–291.

3. W. R. Bion. *Learning from Experience* (London: Heinemann, 1962).

4. C. Noble & R. Coram. *Bridge Across My Sorrows* (London: Transworld Publishers, 1995).

5. D. W. Winnicott. "Ego distortions in terms of true and false self" (1960). In: *The Maturational Processes and the Facilitating Environment* (London: Hogarth Press & The Institute of Psychoanalysis, 1965).

6. S. Baron-Cohen. *The Essential Difference: The Truth about the Male & Female Brain* (London: Allen Lane, 2003).

## Part I

1. W. H. Auden. *A Selection by the Author* (Harmondsworth, Middlesex: Penguin, 1958), p. 91.

## Chapter 2

1. W. S. Condon & L. W. Sander. "Synchrony demonstrated between movements of the neonate and adult speech." *Child Development, 45*(1974): 456–462.

2. E. Nagy & P. Molnar. "Homo imitans or homo provocans" [Abstract]. *International Journal of Psychophysiology, 18* (1994): 128.

3. C. Trevarthen. "Intrinsic motives for companionship in understanding: Their origin, development, and significance for infant mental health." *Infant Mental Health Journal, 22* (2001): 95–131.

4. A. N. Meltzoff & M. K. Moore. "Infant intersubjectivity: Broadening the dialogue to include imitation, identity and intention." In: S. Braten (Ed.), *Intersubjective Communication and Emotion in Early Ontogeny* (Cambridge: Cambridge University Press, 1998), pp. 47–62.

5. A. N. Meltzoff & W. Borton. "Intermodal matching by human neonates." *Nature, 282* (1979): 403–404.

6. A. N. Meltzoff & M. K. Moore. "A theory of the role of imitation in the emergence of self." In: P. Rochat (Ed.), *The Self in Infancy: Theory and Research* (Amsterdam: Elsevier, 1995).

7. M. Scaife & J. S. Bruner. "The capacity for joint visual attention in the human infant." *Nature, 253* (1975): 265.

8. G. Butterworth. "The ontogeny and phylogeny of joint visual attention." In: A. Whiten (Ed.), *Natural Theories of Mind: Evolution, Development and Simulation of Everyday Mindreading* (Oxford: Basil Blackwell, 1991), pp. 223–232.

9. E. M. Forster, *Howards End*, chapter 22.

10. E. Z. Tronick. "Emotions and emotional communication in infants." *American Psychologist, 44* (1989): 112–119.

11. D. N. Stern. *The Interpersonal World of the Infant* (New York: Basic Books, 1985).

12. D. W. Winnicott. "Hate in the countertransference" (1947). In: *Collected Papers: Through Paediatrics to Psychoanalysis* (London: Tavistock Publications, 1958).

### Chapter 3

1. William Wordsworth. "The Two-part Prelude." In: J. Wordsworth (Ed.), *The Pedlar, Tintern Abbey and the Two-part Prelude* (Cambridge: Cambridge University Press, 1985).

2. C. Trevarthen. "Psychobiology of speech development." In: E. Lenneberg (Ed.), *Language and Brain: Developmental Aspects. Neurobiology Sciences Research Program Bulletin, 12* (1974): 570–585.

3. G. Butterworth. "The ontogeny and phylogeny of joint visual attention." In: A. Whiten (Ed.), *Natural Theories of Mind: Evolution, Development and Simulation of Everyday Mindreading* (Oxford: Blackwell, 1991), pp. 223–232.

4. D. J. Siegel. "Towards an interpersonal neurobiology of the developing mind: Attachment relationships, 'Mindsight,' and neural integration." *Infant Mental Health Journal, 22* (2001): 71.

5. A. N. Meltzoff & M. K. Moore. "A theory of the role of imitation in

the emergence of self." In: P. Rochat (Ed.), *The Self in Infancy: Theory and Research* (Amsterdam: Elsevier, 1995).

6. B. Jordan. "Reflux and irritability." In: F. Thomson Salo & C. Paul (Eds.), *The Baby as Subject: New Directions in Infant–Parent Psychotherapy from the Royal Children's Hospital, Melbourne* (Melbourne: Stonnington Press, 2004).

7. J. M. Selby & B. S. Bradley. "Infants in groups: A paradigm for the study of early social experience." *Human Development, 46* (2003): 197–221.

## Chapter 4

1. F. Thomson Salo & C. Paul (Eds.), *The Baby as Subject: New Directions in Infant–Parent Psychotherapy from the Royal Children's Hospital, Melbourne* (Melbourne: Stonnington Press, 2004), p. 13.

2. C. Trevarthen. "The concept and foundations of infant intersubjectivity." In: S. Braten (Ed.), *Intersubjective Communication and Emotion in Early Ontogeny* (Cambridge: Cambridge University Press, 1998), p. 38.

3. F. Pine. "Mahler's concepts of 'Symbiosis' and separation-individuation: Revisited, reevaluated, refined." *Journal of the American Psychoanalytic Association, 52* (2004): 511–533.

4. S. Chess & A. Thomas. *Temperament in Clinical Practice* (New York: Guilford Press, 1986).

5. C. Trevarthen. "Infant psychology is an evolving culture. Commentary on: 'Infants in Groups: A paradigm for the Study of Early Social Development'." *Human Development, 46* (2003): 233–246.

6. F. Thomson Salo. "The interface with infant research: The continuing gains for psychoanalysis." *Psychoanalysis Downunder. The Online Journal of the Australian Psychoanalytical Society, Issue No. 1, July* 2001 (www.psychoanalysisdownunder.com).

7. S. Coates. Discussion point. Conference on Psychoanalysis, Attachment and the Neurosciences, London, 2002.

## Chapter 5

1. N. Tzourio-Mazoyer, S. DeSchonen, F. Crivello, B. Reutter, Y. Aujard, & B. Mazoyer. "Neural correlates of woman face-processing by 2-month-old infants." *NeuroImage, 15* (2002): 454–461.

2. R. Emde & J. F. Sorce. "The rewards of infancy: Emotional availability and social referencing." In: J. D. Call, E. Galenson, & R. L. Tyson (Eds.), *Frontiers of Infant Psychiatry* (New York: Basic Books, 1983).

3. W. R. Bion. "A theory of thinking." *International Journal of Psy-*

*choanalysis, 43* (1962): 306–310 [republished in *Second Thoughts*. London: Heinemann, 1967].

4. A. N. Schore. *Affect Regulation and the Origin of the Self: The Neurobiology of Emotional Development* (Hillsdale, NJ: Lawrence Erlbaum, 1994).

5. Holmes, J. *The Search for the Secure Base: Attachment Theory and Psychotherapy* (Hove: Brunner-Routledge, 2001).

6. Bion, W. R. *Attention and Interpretation* (London: Tavistock, 1970).

7. M. Meehan. "In the nurse's consulting room. I. The experience of weaning: Psychic trauma and relationship disruption." In: F. Thomson Salo & C. Paul (Eds.), *The Baby as Subject: New Directions in Infant–Parent Psychotherapy from the Royal Children's Hospital, Melbourne* (Melbourne: Stonnington Press, 2004).

8. D. W. Winnicott. *Playing and Reality* (London: Tavistock, 1971), pp. 65–85.

9. S. Baron-Cohen. *The Essential Difference: The Truth about the Male & Female Brain* (London: Allen Lane, 2003), p. 33.

10. D. W. Winnicott. "The capacity to be alone" (1958). In: *The Maturational Processes and the Facilitating Environment* (London: Hogarth Press & The Institute of Psychoanalysis, 1965).

## Part II

1. Quoted in D. W. Winnicott, *Playing and Reality* (London: Tavistock, 1971), p. 95.

## Chapter 6

1. O. Gaverieux. "The internal and external parental couple." *Infant Observation, 5* (2002): 39–55.

2. S. Baron-Cohen. *The Essential Difference: The Truth about the Male & Female Brain* (London: Allen Lane, 2003), p. 89.

3. O. Gaverieux. "The internal and external parental couple." *Infant Observation, 5* (2002): 39–55.

4. E. Goldschmied & D. Selleck. *Communication between Babies in Their First Year* [video] (London: National Children's Bureau Enterprises, 1986).

5. E. C. Mueller & D. Vandell. "Infant–infant interaction." In: J. D. Osofsky (Ed.), *Handbook of Infant Development*, 1st edition (New York: Wiley, 1979).

## Chapter 7

1. J. J. McKenna. "Cultural influences on infant and childhood sleep biology, and the science that studies it: Towards a more inclusive

paradigm." In: J. Loughlin, J. Carroll, & C. Marcus (Eds.), *Sleep and Breathing in Children: A Developmental Approach* (New York: Marcel Dekker, 2000), pp. 199–230.

2. A. Bharucha. "Multiple mothering in an Indian context." In: F. Thomson Salo (Ed.), *Mothers and Infants: New Perspectives* (Melbourne: Stonnington Press, 2003).

3. D. W. Winnicott. "Transitional objects and transitional phenomena." In: *Playing and Reality* (London: Tavistock, 1971).

4. Sue Morse, personal communication, 2004.

Chapter 8

1. A. Morgan, personal communication, 2004.

2. L. Murray. "Intersubjectivity, object relations theory, and empirical evidence from mother–infant interactions." *Infant Mental Health Journal, 12* (1991): 219–232.

3. G. Butterworth. "The ontogeny and phylogeny of joint visual attention." In: A. Whiten (Ed.), *Natural Theories of Mind: Evolution, Development and Simulation of Everyday Mindreading* (Oxford: Basil Blackwell, 1991), pp. 223–232.

4. S. Dehaene (http://www.sciencentral.com/articles/view.php3?type=article&article_id=218392324), accessed 2 October 2004

5. P. K. Kuhl. "Language, culture, and intersubjectivity: The creation of shared perception." In: S. Braten (Ed.), *Intersubjective Communication and Emotion in Early Ontogeny* (Cambridge: Cambridge University Press, 1998), pp. 297–315.

6. K. Cooke, personal communication, 2003.

7. D. N. Stern. *The Interpersonal World of the Infant* (New York: Basic Books, 1985).

8. Sue Morse, personal communication, 2004.

9. N. Akhtar & M. Tomasello. "Intersubjectivity in early language learning and use." In: S. Braten (Ed.), *Intersubjective Communication and Emotion in Early Ontogeny* (Cambridge: Cambridge University Press, 1998), pp. 316–335.

Chapter 9

1. D. W. Winnicott. "Transitional objects and transitional phenomena." In: *Playing and Reality* (London: Tavistock, 1971).

Chapter 10

1. A. H. Brafman. *Can You Help Me? A Guide for Parents* (London: Karnac, 2004).

2. F. Grier. "Amanda: Observations and reflections of a bottle-fed

baby who found a breast mother." In: J. Raphael-Leff (Ed.), *Parent–Infant Psychodynamics: Wild things, mirrors and ghosts* (London: Whurr, 2003), pp. 209–230.

3. M. Klein. "The Oedipus complex in the light of early anxieties" (1945). In: *The Writings of Melanie Klein, Vol. 1* (London: Hogarth Press, 1975), pp. 370–419.

4. S. Hart, T. Field, & C. Del Valle. "Infants protest their mothers' attending to an infant-size doll." *Social Development, 7* (1998): 54–61.

Part III

1. Alfred, Lord Tennyson. *In Memoriam A.H.H.*, LIV: 5.

Chapter 11

1. C. Paul. "Sick Babies—The Role of the Infant Psychiatrist in the Midst of Life, Death and Survival." RANZCP Faculty of Child & Adolescent Psychiatry Annual Meeting, Darwin, Australia, 2004.

2. L. W. Sander, G. Stechler, P. Burns, & A. Lee. "Change in infant and caregiver variables over the first two months of life: Integration of action in early development." In: E. B. Thoman (Ed.), *Origins of the Infant's Social Responsiveness* (Hillsdale, NJ: Lawrence Erlbaum, 1979).

3. S. Fraiberg. *Clinical Studies in Infant Mental Health: The First Year of Life* (London: Tavistock Publications, 1980).

4. S. Abrams, T. Field, F. Scafidi, & M. Prodromidis. "Newborns of depressed mothers." *Infant Mental Health Journal, 16* (1995): 233–239.

5. The nursing staff, Monash Medical Centre Mother–Baby Unit, personal communication.

6. S. Fraiberg. *Clinical Studies in Infant Mental Health: The First Year of Life* (London: Tavistock Publications, 1980).

7. F. Thomson Salo & C. Paul (Eds.), *The Baby as Subject: New Directions in Infant–Parent Psychotherapy from the Royal Children's Hospital, Melbourne* (Melbourne: Stonnington Press, 2004), p. 16.

adopted babies, 111–112
aggression, 35
air swallowing, 127
ambivalence, 51–52
    babies', to other babies, 52, 76
    parents', in relationship with
        baby, 8, 19, 83
anger, 51–52
annihilation, fear of, 7
anxiety(ies):
    babies', 7–8, 16, 45, 50–51, 59, 114
        fear of separation, 8
        fear of strangers, 86
        fear of threat to survival, 109
    memories of, 6
    and splitting off bad aspects, 8
attachment, 2, 17, 58, 94, 98, 102, 108
    and capacity for self-reflective
        function, 93
    insecure, 79–81
    problems of babies in hospital,
        110–111
    secure, 9, 23, 79–81, 101
    and separation, 77–88
    theory, 4
attention deficit hyperactivity
        disorder, 114
attunement, 56, 57
Auden, W. H., 12
autism, 131
autonomy, babies' developing sense
        of, 29, 48, 52
    and saying "no", 34

bereavement, baby born after, 112
bodily pleasures, 41–43
body mapping, 41–43
bottle-feeding, 61, 95, 124, 127–128
    weaning from, 83
breastfeeding, 16, 27–30, 39, 50, 60,
        84–85, 95, 124, 126, 127–
        128
    example, 27–28
    see also: bottle-feeding; feeding;
        spoonfeeding; weaning

childbirth, medicalization of, 123
child care, 87–88
Coates, Susan, 53
colic, 31
communication:
    babies':
        nonverbal, parents'
            understanding of, 18–19
        predisposition for, 24–26
            examples, 25–26
        breakdown of, 93
        crying as, 30–31
        emotional, 25, 64
            example, 61–62
        through eyes, 58–60
        intersubjective, 55
            of feelings, 60–62
            triadic, 32
        visual example, 33
concern for others, capacity for,
        development of, 3, 98–105

conscience, development of, 103–104
containment, parental, of babies' feelings, 59
coping, 116–118
creativity, 9
    baby's, 27, 86, 96
        example, 29
    of play, 9, 29
crying, 10
    and air swallowing, 127
    as communication, 7, 30–31, 59, 83
    in distress, 129
    in empathy, 10
    at night, 83
    when separated from parent, 79

depressed babies, 114, 119
    example, 120
depressed mother, 72, 76, 113–115
    example, 65
depressive position, 99
developing self, 9–10
developmental milestones, 128–129
disability, 109–120
disintegration, 118
dissociation, 117–118
distress, communicating:
    via crying, 30
    via psychosomatic language, 7
dummy, 16, 38, 85
    see also: thumb sucking
dynamic system, 59

empathy/empathic self, 3, 12, 17, 55, 76, 103
    baby's, 55–66
        gender differences in, 63
enjoyment in being enjoyed, 17–18
expectancies, development of, 56–57
extended family, 74–75
eye contact, 26, 100
    avoidance of, 49, 116

face recognition, 43
failure to thrive:
    and "ghost in the nursery", 40
    and anxieties, 50
fantasies and anxieties, 50–51

father(s), 98
    relationship with, example, 70
    role of, 69–72
    support to mother during weaning, 84
    see also: mother(s); parent(s)
feeding, 27–29, 124
    difficulties, 83–85
    and hunger, 30, 45
    see also: bottle-feeding; breastfeeding; weaning
feelings:
    and emotional relationship, 93
    expression of, 65
    relational, complex, 47–49
    words as containers of, 93
finger food, 28
forgiveness, 102
fostered babies, 111–112
frustration, 34–35

gag reflex, 10
gender:
    developing sense of, 9–10
    differences:
        in development of speech, 93
        in empathy, 63, 66
        in relationship with depressed mother, 114
        in weaning, 84
    see also: sex differences
"ghosts in the nursery", 19, 21, 80, 113, 115
grandparents, 74
gratitude, 103

hurt, 49–50
hypervigilance, 117–118

identification:
    babies':
        with father, 71
        with others, 62, 71
        with parent, 99
    parents', with child, 72
illness, 109–120
illusion, 95
imitation, 26
immunization, 130
impulsivity, 35
individuation, 87

infant–parent psychotherapy, 118–131
inner world, babies', 89–90
intentional self/intentionality, baby's, 3, 12, 17, 24–36
intersubjectivity, 14
  neurobiological basis for, 55
  primary, 24

jealousy, 48, 72, 73, 74, 100, 102

language, babies' understanding of, 92–94

magical thinking, 95–96
masturbation, 42
meaning, search of baby's mind for, 6–7
memories, babies', parents holding, 53–54
mirroring:
  babies', 14, 25, 55, 90
  mother's, 25, 58, 78
miscarriage, 20, 112
mother (*passim*):
  absent, 92
  baby's coherent view of, 37
  depressed, 72, 76, 113–115
    example, 65
  gaze of, 58–60
  good internal, 9
  separation from, 87
  *see also:* father(s); parent(s)
musicality, dialogue of, 79
musical play, 42

"nameless dread", 7
narcissism:
  healthy, 95–97
  and self-esteem, 96–97
newborns, knowledge and abilities of, 13–17
Newman, Claus G. H., 123–131
Noble, Christina, 9
normality, babies', 124–126

object constancy, 78
oedipal stage, 99–102
  difficulties in, 102–103
oedipal wishes, 98–105
Oedipus, myth of, 99–102

omnipotence, 95–97

pain, 109–120
  communicating:
    via crying, 30
    via psychosomatic language, 7
parent(s):
  anger of, as cause of anxiety, 8
  attributions of, 19–21
  contribution of, 18–19
  emotional holding-in-mind by, 53
  –infant relationship, co-constructing, 21–22
  interaction of, 32
  loving internal, 8–9
  naming feelings, 93–94
  reverie of, 57
  sleep deprivation of, 22
  thinking mind of
    babies' need for, 57–58
  *see also:* father(s); mother(s)
peek-a-boo game, 44, 76, 85
play:
  alone, capacity for, 64
  creative, example, 29
  musical, 42
  symbolic, 30
  teasing as, 63
playfulness:
  adult's, 92
  baby's, 29–30
post-traumatic stress disorder, 113
potential space, 86
pregnancy, 5, 125
  medicalization of, 123
primary maternal preoccupation, 5
procedural memory system, 6
projection:
  by baby, of ideas and feelings, 8
  parents', onto baby, 19
proprioceptive information, 14
psychosomatic body, 39–40
psychosomatic language of babies, 7
psychotherapy, infant–parent, 118–131
puerperium, disorganization of, 5

reality-testing, 8
reflective function, baby's, 93
reparation, 99
reverie, parental, 57

rivalry, sibling, 72

saying "no", 34–35
secrets, 61, 94
self:
    achievements of, 64
    developing, 9–10
        first two months, 13–23
self-comforting, 37–38
self-consciousness, 40–41
self-differentiation, 43–44
self-esteem, 3, 18, 23, 42, 47
    developing, 96–97
self-recognition, baby's, 37–54
self-reflective function, babies', and
        attachment, 93
selfishness and unselfishness,
        struggle between, 99
separation, 27, 49, 74
    and attachment, 77–88
    of baby into individual, 20
    coping with, 3
    experience of, 77–78
    from mother, 87
sex differences, 10, 63
    see also: gender differences
shame, 49–50
siblings, 3, 22, 28, 72–74, 98
sleep deprivation, parents', 22
sleeping, 81–83
smiling, 38–39
social referencing, 55
"social smile", 130
splitting off bad aspects, 8
spoonfeeding, 28
    see also: bottle-feeding;
        breastfeeding; feeding;
        weaning
stranger-anxiety, 86

teasing, 49, 62–63
temperament:
    babies', 18, 20, 44–46, 80
        "difficult", 44, 46, 80, 81, 85,
        111

"easy", 44
Tennyson, Alfred, Lord, 108
thinking, 89–94
    example, 91
    in utero, 90
    magical, 95–96
    processes, development of, 3
thinking mind, parents', babies'
        need for, 57–58
three-way relationship, baby and
        parents, example, 100–101
thumb sucking as self-comforting,
        42–43
    see also: dummy
time, sense of, 91–92
toilet training, 104
transitional object(s), 85–86, 88,
        110
transitional space, 86
trauma:
    from parents' past, 113
    in relationship, 115–116
traumatic events, babies' response
        to, 111, 112–113
Trevarthen, Colwyn, 47
twins, 73–74
    jealousy in, 100

Uganda, 4

value system, development of, 103–
        104

walking, 35–36
weaning, 62, 84
    difficulties, 83–85
        example, 61–62
    see also: bottle-feeding;
        breastfeeding; feeding;
        spoonfeeding
weight gain, 126–127
Winnicott, Donald, 1, 19, 68
words as containers of feelings, 93
Wordsworth, William, 24
"wrappedness of attention", 58

Made in United States
North Haven, CT
15 December 2022

29121186R00088